THE RABID WATCHDOGS

THE RABID WATCHDOGS

ABUSES WITHIN OUR IMPERFECT
WORLD:REFLECTIONS OF
A PSYCHOTHERAPIST

MARY D. MORGILLO

XULON PRESS

Xulon Press
2301 Lucien Way #415
Maitland, FL 32751
407.339.4217
www.xulonpress.com

Unless otherwise indicated, Scripture quotations taken from The Catholic Press, Inc.— Old Testament in the Douay-Challoner Text, New Testament in Confraternity Text, 1951

Printed in the United States of America.

ISBN-13: 9781545650721

This book is dedicated to my late husband, "Connie," who stood by my side through the good times and the bad times for over forty years and who shared the pain of the nightmare chronicled within these pages. I could not have survived the betrayal without him even though I fervently wish it had not accelerated his death so that we could have enjoyed our old age together. Nonetheless, his memory will ever be an inspiration. I also want to express my heartfelt appreciation for the support, encouragement, and help I received from my family and my friends in the writing of my experience.

Note: The names of persons involved in the nightmare (except for Connie and me) have been changed to protect the innocent.

CONTENTS

———✳———

MARY D. MORGILLO

INTRODUCTION

———————— ✳ ————————

*F*rom the time I had experienced the effects of the betrayal and lost my trust in others (especially government personnel and attorneys) until the time I believed writing this book was a need, I read more about the abuses of Medicaid and the health care crisis in general. One of the gifts of this humbling experience was to teach me not to be judgmental of anyone's interpretation of another's behavior, even my own. There was pain in the recognition I might not have paid careful attention to such outcries had I not tasted the bitterness of dishonesty directed at me. I realized I, too, had thought accounts of being wrongly accused of fraud, overcharging, and excesses of treatment were exaggerated. Moreover, that someone could be falsely accused of these "crimes" without reason never occurred to me. The belief there could be unjust provocation for suspecting an employer or a professional was part of my naiveté. I had no idea, for example, that the Medifraud office encouraged, supported, and embellished accusations of employees who had personal vendettas against an employee, especially mental health professionals in private practice. The reasons for this were obvious. The services rendered were not easily described and measured as were other health services, individual private practitioners would not be financially able to defend themselves, and the public's scrutiny of the Medicare/Medicaid system would be diverted. That irreparable harm to doctors' reputations, doctor-patient relationships, and the mental health of millions had not been considered.

As more and more articles about Medifraud accusations caught my attention, it was apparent I had had my head in the sand. While I knew that fraud was being committed and needed to be properly investigated, I had not recognized there were many that were wrongly accused or being set up to be falsely investigated. The happy endings for the wrongly accused portrayed on television stories are often fantasies. I knew of no Jessica Fletchers, Perry Masons, Matlocks, or real-life attorneys willing to work without compensation to promote truth or justice or cause. (Most would claim to be unable to afford donating sufficient time or resources to do so.) Yet, they continued to urge health care professionals to donate skills and time to care for the elderly, neglected, and poor, knowing full well the volunteers would be increasing their risks of malpractice lawsuits and charges of fraud. The handbook regarding the mandatory reporting of abuse while treating these populations, for example, states that if sued or charged with fraud, the doctor should not panic but must engage the services of an attorney immediately.

Writing this book had several purposes as time went on. The initial need to bring healing to me and those close to me who had been injured by the false accusations of a few vindictive employees remained one of the primary reasons. Others almost as important emerged. I wanted healing for myself and for my husband, who stood by my side throughout the entire ordeal; unfortunately, he died before he saw an end to the injustices against me. Nonetheless, the memories of his love and support have helped me get through the pain of betrayal even after his death. I wanted to write a memorial to those who died because of being similarly victimized and whose hearts gave out before they saw any light at the end of this dark tunnel. I also wanted to alert fellow practitioners of their vulnerability. Many of the doctors who lent me their support encouraged me to write a book about my experiences because they had found them both unbelievable and frightening. They doubted most health practitioners were aware than anyone could make a false accusation resulting their being treated as guilty until proven innocent, while relentless government prosecutors forced costs of defending oneself into hundreds of thousands of dollars. Few can afford the high cost of defending themselves in any suit involving a government agency. As the talk about promoting a national health care coverage plan intensified and more managed health care organizations emerged, my alarm increased. I knew the public was aware there were abuses by recipients and providers, but did they have any idea of the major abuses within? I doubted this and was certain my story could alert others of the importance of careful examination of their office reimbursement management and procedures. This book, then, addresses aspects of the Medicare/Medicaid system and the contradictory legalities that protected it at the time when the travesty of justice I experienced took place. Before the reader gets an incorrect perception of the intent of this statement, let me stress there are legitimate concerns regarding abuses of health care systems; however, there can be greater abuses taking place within the structures set up to regulate and protect them. Many insurance programs have a "pyramid structure." The monies collected benefit the administrators at the top much more than the recipients on the bottom. Thus, before we give greater control to government officials or managed health care organizations for developing and managing national health care plans, it is prudent to examine carefully an established system.

The numerous articles appearing in magazines, journals, and newspapers usually focused on the abuses and fraud committed by the providers of health care, especially the abuses and fraud of Medicare/Medicaid monies. There were national television stories and exposés that also did this. A few, such as Diane Sawyer on *Primetime*, professional journals, and professional newspapers were willing to expose the administrators of the programs as well. As these few came out with the less popular side, major magazines such as *Newsweek*, *Time*, and *Modern Maturity* seemed to be trying to counteract any possibility administrators of these programs could be a major source of wrongdoing. What they published sometimes sounded like propaganda fed to them by insurers. Although my experience has produced a lack of respect of and trust in much of our legal system, this disdain will not deter my belief in the moral values with which I live my life. My faith provided strength; I knew I was innocent. However, I could not have endured the pain of this nightmarish experience without my love of God and my faith He would always be at my side. It was the guiding light which aided me in truly forgiving all who were instrumental in bringing about the nightmare. I believe most of the players were unaware of the consequences of their actions and thought they were justified to do what they did. Nonetheless, I wonder what happens to those who were not fortunate enough to have the early exposure to a moral, ethical environment such as the religious one in which I grew up. I no longer wonder why the crime rate has increased as the lack of morality, religiousness, and family values have decreased in our society. I recognize history tends to repeat itself, and the lessons taught in *The Rise and Fall of Rome* may have to be retaught before our country returns to the ideals on which our forefathers built it.

As the story of what happened to me unfolds, it is my hope the reader will keep an open mind and look at both sides of the problem before it is too late to stop the tide of an explosive system out of control. The answer is not in giving more power to insurance companies or government agencies with their numerous bureaucratic levels. When dealing with any governing body, one must remember the words of Lord Acton, who wrote in the last half of the nineteenth century, "Power tends to corrupt and absolute power corrupts absolutely."

CHAPTER ONE

SETTING THE STAGE

———— ✳ ————

"How could this be? Is it history repeating itself? Is this a nightmare?" These were the questions I asked myself when the tragic experience happened. Yet even when it occurred, I knew it was different because reality stared at me in the face, and I was no longer a child. Yet, I saw my father's face and heard my mother's sobs all over again. His partner and his best friend (or so he thought) had emptied his company's bank account. My dad became a rock of courage for me as I recalled what he and my mom had gone through so many years before. My dad, a tool and die maker for a stamping company, had lost three of the fingers and part of those knuckles on his right hand in a horrible punch press accident at work. The surgeon told him he would never be able to work at his trade again. My dad replied, "Watch me." He had most of his thumb and bottom two phalanges of his little finger. He kept bringing them together until, weeks later, he was able to pick up things with them. The doctors were amazed. However, no one would hire him. During his recovery, he helped build the home I grew up in. Later on, my mom went to work and my dad continued "playing" with his tools. He began inventing household items (things such as a banana bunch holder, a spare toilet tissue roll holder that looked like a cat, a tiny sleigh in which to place Christmas cards, a miniature rocking chair for spools of thread that had a cushion for needles and pins, etc.). People began asking for these gadgets. He also was inventing tools and designed and built television towers for better television reception. They showed up on many homes once he had produced them in quantity. In short, he started his own tool shop in a cement building he built next to the home he had built for his family. My mom happily quit her factory job when World War II was over. She became the bookkeeper and office manager. He hired a few people, including a man he had known as his best friend since his childhood and who became his partner. Things looked bright for a few years until that terrible day. But my father retained his optimism and even forgave his friend years later. He and my mom weathered that storm.

My parents married shortly after the depression had overtaken this country. They had no money, and their extended families were having problems surviving as were many other rural families at that time. They did, however, have strong religious, moral, and work ethics as well as a belief that most people valued the same integrity and trustworthiness they had. They passed these beliefs on to me and my younger two sisters. The personal sacrifices and struggles of many North Americans during the first half of the twentieth century were much harder than portrayed romantically in novels and television dramas. My father had lost his job because of the depression and just before their planned wedding in April. They married anyway, and with the help of family, they rented a small home. Both had been raised on farms, so they planted a garden, and my mother put up food to sustain them through the winter months. My father picked up coal along the train tracks to warm the home and did odd jobs for the money they needed for other essentials. My mother became pregnant with me that fall. I now know they were worried about having a baby when they were so poor; again, they trusted God to help them.

As time for my birth neared, my mother and her sisters prepared the home, and my mother made a baby layette from feed sacks. Of course, my aunts expected to assist the birthing process because they had no money for a physician to do that. However, my mother was having a difficult time, so my father rushed to get a physician. I finally arrived with the cord around my neck and had to be pushed back into the birth canal. I can honestly say I was born twice. I was in trouble, but the physician was able to revive me. My mother said he told her I would have some problems due to the trauma. That did not faze her; she maintained I was a fighter. My diet was restricted because I would break out in a rash if I ate wheat products. I did not know about my birth until I had a difficult time having my own daughter. Six months into my pregnancy, I became very sick and was confined to bedrest. Connie took me to stay with my mother for about six weeks so that my mother could care for me and our infant son. One of my symptoms was hemosiderosis. In my old bedroom was a copy of Heinrich Hofmann's portrait of Jesus in the Garden of Gethsemane. As Mom sat with me one day, we talked about the blessing I had received. This was our response to my comment to her that I was being asked to share in Our Savior's Agony so I could not complain about my lesser sufferings. It was then she shared my birth trauma. I also remember her telling me, when I had pneumonia as a teenager, that I would have to fight to stay healthy all my life. I also had learned to live with heart and lung problems and difficulty with anemia and gaining weight until I reached middle age.

I never fully appreciated the legacies passed on to me while growing up. I remember only briefly being ashamed of the feed sack dresses my mother had lovingly made for me because joyful memories of family and friends overshadowed them. Most people in our community were also struggling, so sharing what you had with others was normal. One of the gifts I had been blessed with was the ability to learn. From very early in life, books were available to me, and I had learned to read before starting grade school. I am sure, in the beginning, I was motivated by the scene of my father relaxing after a hard day's work with a book in his hands. As I reflect on the memories of my parents and my two sisters being a family, my admiration of and my respect for my parents grows. I have recollections of extended family functions, reunions, and friendships with many cousins. I remember how neighbors looked out for and helped each other. Nostalgia for the past sustains my present.

I went to a one-room public school, all eight grades with one teacher, until the end of fourth grade. The school burned down that summer. Our parish church was built then, and I started fifth grade in the basement of the church until it was finished. The classes were much larger, and there were two grades for every teacher. The school was a little over a mile from our home, but all of us on that road walked to school daily, even in the coldest deep snow. Yet, we laughed and enjoyed each other to and from school. It was a simple but very fulfilling life. During that time, I decided I wanted to become a nun. One of the nuns talked to my parents about a preparatory boarding high school, and I wrote a letter applying to go there. I received a scholarship for my freshman year. It was near Grand Rapids, Michigan. I had never lived that far away from home before. During the winter, I became very sick with pneumonia. Mother Superior took me in her office one day. She told me my health problems prohibited her from recommending me to stay in the aspirational program for another year. Her words stung deeply: "Some girls are meant to join the convent and teach; others, like you, are meant to marry and have the children to teach." My parents could not afford to pay the tuition for me to continue high school at the academy, so I entered the public high school in the fall.

Even so, the dream of helping others had been a lifetime dream. I considered becoming a physician; however, not all doors (in particular, those of medical schools) were open to women when I graduated from high school. So, I followed the expectations of the time and married young, right out of high school, the man to whom I remained married for over forty years until his death. Our first son was born when I was twenty years old. A year later, we had our daughter. The pregnancy was a difficult one, and I had heart failure during her birth. I vividly recall the experience of dying and being brought back to life. It changed me in so many ways and strengthened my faith. I was very grateful for the nurse who visited me during the hospitalization after my daughter was born. Being fearful someone would say it was just a dream, she verified the experience. She said she wanted to see me because she had witnessed a miracle in the delivery room. She stated, "We lost you, but the doctor brought you back. I had to see for myself that you and your daughter are doing well." I was able to endure a miscarriage a few months after this. Our third child, a son, was born a year after the miscarriage; my pregnancy with him was without problems. I became pregnant three times after his birth but was unable to carry the babies beyond three months.

As more and more doors opened to women, Connie and I were busy raising our three wonderful children. Nonetheless, I realized I was not content with the traditional role of a homemaker as my children approached school age and the time and physical demands of caring for our young children diminished. Someone suggested taking an adult education course at the university when I mentioned a desire to write for publication. School had been a source of satisfaction to me in the past. I enjoyed reading about new things and learning about the world in general. Since I usually did not spend much time watching daytime television or reading romance-type novels, the suggestion intrigued me. I enrolled in a creative writing class. Being exposed to higher education was a gratifying undertaking and, with the instructor's encouragement, I enrolled in a baccalaureate program. After discerning objectives and interests, I decided to register in an elementary education program. I had little idea then of the difficulties I would face as a nontraditional student or of the sacrifices I and my family would have to make for me to obtain a bachelor of education. Because I had enjoyed science and mathematics in high school, I choose them as my major fields of study along with English. It was not unusual to be one of a few females in large classes of males; sometimes there were debasing remarks made about this but I paid little attention to any undercurrent of prejudice. I belonged to two honor societies and was elected to several officer positions by fellow students. This boosted my self-esteem and I felt accepted by them.

Although I recognized it was more difficult for a wife and mother to obtain a college degree as I obtained an undergraduate degree, I had not experienced the rejection of prejudice until I decided to go to graduate school at the University of Toledo. I had never taken a college course until my three children were in grade school, and becoming a teacher seemed acceptable to the majority of professors I encountered in undergraduate courses. Obtaining a dual major in English and in science and mathematics, I proceeded to apply for pre-med so that I eventually could be a psychiatrist.

The door to med school was closed to mothers with children then; the prevailing idea was that a mother's commitment should be to her children and med school required too much of a commitment for women with children. A few years later, as I grew beyond the age when the doors closed to both men and women, this changed. No matter, I accepted this; I saw value in the earlier concern for children and in my own commitment to my family. By this time, I had decided to help people grow to their greatest potential through teaching and counseling and completed a master's program in guidance and counseling. Therein began a prejudicial struggle. The prejudicial treatment and discrimination directed toward women in academia and in professional fields exists yet today. Several major newspapers across the country have reported this frequently. *The Blade*, a Toledo-area newspaper, for example, on December 16, 1993, reported that a sex and age discrimination suit was filed against the University of Toledo by a woman who was a tenured professor and director of the university's medical assisting program.

I soon recognized a school counselor (then) was more of a scheduler than the counselor I had envisioned a counselor to be. So, my desire to help others became a quest to become a psychologist, which required a doctorate degree in my state. During my academic career, financial aid was not available to me. Women were considered dependents of their husband if husband and wife filed a joint federal income tax return. In the majority of cases, most women working outside the home made less than their husbands, and financial penalties of filing separate federal tax returns outweighed the benefits. Regardless, my husband made slightly more than the allowable limit for a dependent to apply for such aid. In addition, at that time, no consideration for child care or homemaking tasks was given. I was required to hold down a fulltime teaching job to pay for my education. Many of the master's degree courses I had taken were the same courses the psychology majors took even though my master in guidance and counseling was awarded through the Education Department of the University. Thus, when the Clinical Psychology Department would not allow any of my Master's degree courses to be credited toward a doctorate in that department, there was no way I could afford to throw away four years' hard work without financial aid. Although I came to realize it was a part of academic politics, repeating courses still does not make sense when one has attained passing grades, especially As. According to the State Board rules then, I would be able to take the State Board Examination if I had a doctorate with a major in psychology, and I would be able to take the specialty oral examination in clinical psychology if I had taken the prescribed courses. Thus, my dissertation and doctorate program were designed with this in mind. Even so, I would have many more hours in my doctorate than most clinical psychology students, but I would not have to repeat courses previously taken, and my doctorate would be awarded by the College of Education. I was given the assurance that, passing the State Board Examination and becoming licensed, I would be allowed to do that which my goals prepared me to do. (I forgot to mention I had been a dreamer by nature as well as a believer in the goodness of all persons.)

One hurdle after another was thrown in my way, primarily by two psychology professors who did not want the field to be opened to women and who would continue to be allowed to interfere in my career even after I had graduated. They attempted to block any attempts I made to practice as the clinical psychologist I was trained to be. The clinical director of the psychology program wrote letters prohibiting me from being listed in the National Register because I had not received all my education from the psychology department even though I had taken a much more robust clinical psychology major than others in the psychology department had taken. In addition, I had taken several post-doctorate courses, workshops, and seminars in clinical psychology to expand my knowledge and skills even further. The irony of it was the two professors who tried to make my life miserable had received their licenses through a grandfather clause while I had taken the extensive board examination. My husband and I made a trip to Columbus to discuss with a Board officer (and a clinical psychologist) my frustrations with the tactics of the director of the University's clinical psychology department. He was sympathetic and said my preparation was much more extensive than his own. He also told me something should be done to stop the unfair tactics, he would write the National Register himself, and I would obtain proper recognition for my preparation. As far as I know, he did nothing. I learned another member of the Board may have curtailed his efforts. Was it just a coincidence? The other professor from the university was a member of the Board. Although being listed in the National Register was important for professional recognition and financial benefits, I still would be able to practice my vocation as a psychotherapist and psychodiagnostician. Therefore, neither my husband nor I felt the aggravation and expense of fighting for the listing were worth it.

The game played with my professional life was a result of "politics" between the Departments of Education and Psychology. Less one believes these statements are the ramblings of a discontented psychotherapist, there were several suits filed by others experiencing the harassment being addressed. They were treated miserably by the press and peers; and all, but one left the area emotionally and professionally bankrupt. I came home one evening in tears after the director told me that I belonged at home with my family, that I would be partially responsible for putting women in the psychology profession, which would lower the range of income of the profession, and that he would one day force me out of the field. I elected not to sue for discrimination because of what had happened to at least three women I knew from the university who had sued. They were "forced" to move to another state by the continued harassment they experienced after their suits were settled out of court, despite the fact the judgments were in their favor. It is my understanding the current situation at universities has improved, but much still needs to be done to lessen the impacts of disparity between men and women professionally and academically.

In addition, it seemed many persons in my chosen profession were afraid of competition from others in psychology, from the medical profession, and from the legal considerations of the State Board. I was to learn, rather than being composed only of persons who would support, encourage, and assist psychologists to become better practitioners by raising their own standards, the Board at that time had become a camouflage for a few who were on ego trips, who needed to play power games, and who enjoyed policing techniques of fear. Looking back, I realize my timidity to sue the director of the program and the professor who would continue to harass me, along with my inability to be assertive, were factors in setting the stage for others to emotionally use and abuse me. Today, I find it sad and detestable that many believe it takes a lawsuit to stop the inappropriate behaviors of some; I would prefer to find other methods. Yet many do not sue or turn to the legal community to stop abuse because of legal costs. Even so, I have come to understand the fear of being sued keeps many from settling disputes through communication or mediation. Not being able to confront others I perceived as authority figures, although a part of childhood conditioning, was reinforced during my vocational preparation years. It would prevent me during my private practice years from confronting passive-aggressive employees, thereby giving them permission to continue inappropriate behaviors. It enabled peers and my attorney to easily convince me they knew better than I about employment, legal, and supervision procedures even though I ultimately had the major responsibility for the consequences. The respect for authority my upbringing had instilled within me reinforced my trust in governmental and legal agents; this was reinforced by my naiveté with the Medicare/Medicaid system.

Nevertheless, I completed my doctoral program in psychology six years after obtaining a master of education in guidance and counseling and twenty years after beginning my quest to be a mental health professional. The sacrifices for me and my family were many. I had pursued my education, graduating with honors, at the same time I had worked two full-time jobs, teacher and homemaker. I had applied for and received clinical internships on my own at a social service agency and a residential treatment facility for children. After graduation I obtained a clinical externship at the medical college hospital, which had inpatient and outpatient programs. Thus, when my supervisors encouraged me to take my board examination in clinical psychology, I willingly, unquestioningly, and enthusiastically did so. Not only did I pass at my first attempt, but I did so with a higher score than many who had graduated from the department of psychology. Imagine my surprise when I was told I could not consider myself as well prepared as colleagues who had taken identical courses as I had, but whose degrees were awarded via one professor's approval.

9

Although he had been unable to prevent me and three other women caught up in this academic political game from receiving our degrees, he continued to try to make our lives miserable. Even so, I continued to take post-graduate courses, workshops, and seminars to learn as much as I could and to remain current with the state of the art of my profession. I enjoyed the respect I received from colleagues and was humbly surprised when I was unanimously elected to be the founding president of the Toledo Academy of Professional Psychology.

My genuine concern and care for others paid off in a successful private practice. Again, I attributed my success to my faith. I prayed for my patients when saying the office of Christian Prayer each morning and asked Our Lord to guide my work. Working about sixty hours a week, my caseload filled quickly, and referrals through satisfied patients and referring physicians kept it filled. I promised my husband I would not work more than sixty hours a week, so we could have some quality time together. This would allow me to cover overhead expenses and make a modest salary of about thirty thousand dollars a year. Becoming rich or amassing a fortune was not one of my goals. I put several thousand dollars aside each of the following five years for the time when my husband could retire, and I would be the major provider of our living expenses. Meanwhile, my husband and I lived frugally on his salary while saving mine.

As the patient load increased and my practice became more successful, I began to consider joining forces with someone else. With that thought in mind, the dream of a clinic-type practice was born. I looked for other therapists with similar values and concern for others as my own and who would enjoy working in a team-approach practice. This would allow each therapist to specialize in particular areas, which ultimately would benefit patients. Besides, when one therapist was out of the office for vacation, illness, conferences, or some other reason, there would be someone with knowledge of them available to patients. This would require more support personnel as well. The stage was set for the tragedy coming into my life as I pursued the dream of sharing skills, talents, and good fortune with others, those employed by the clinic and those served by the clinic.

CHAPTER TWO

PRIVATE PRACTICE

*S*o, it was. With "Big Brother" always looking over one's shoulder, with the fear of many psychologists to support each other, with passive-aggressive personalities in the profession abounding, and with a few attempting to form exclusive clubs of psychologists, I began private practice. I had been working in a social service agency as head of the department of psychological services for a couple of years. However, it became uncomfortable to remain in an agency where prejudice toward women was evident, where I felt the jealousy of a few misogynistic males and the envy of some women, and where I witnessed persons on public assistance programs getting second-class treatment. So, I accepted the kind offer to rent space from another psychologist, who demonstrated behaviors more in keeping with the values I had. This decision was further prompted when another department director made disparaging remarks about agency clients. Two years after joining my colleague, it was apparent my caseload was increasing, and it was unfair that he should shoulder the added expense of office personnel to manage all my patients as well as his. So, with his blessing and good wishes, I opened my own office.

Opening the door to my private practice seemed to be the essence of the American dream for me. My husband lent his support in the background and expressed his pride in my achievements as I began my professional work. He shared my joy whenever my efforts brought about behaviors and attitudes that increased the happiness of others. I was pleased when the skills and talents I had spent years developing gained me the reputation of being a Christian psychologist who genuinely cared for the people she was privileged to help. As time went on, whenever I hired someone, a criterion was that they would share this philosophy. Shortly after I opened up my office, Marvin came to work with me part time to earn some extra money. I had known him for twelve years, been his supervisor for several years at the social services agency where we both had worked. He had the same misgivings about the agency as I had had. He began having difficulties with the director of the agency and was let go. Since his caseload had sufficiently built up, he requested the opportunity to work for me full time as a social worker. It would take some of the interview work off me, and he could work under my supervision, so I readily agreed.

A year later I met Darrell, who was director of an agency delivering inner-city assistance. I provided psychological consultation and some therapy for the agency. I was impressed with what I believed he had been able to do with volunteers and a small budget. As our work together continued, he expressed his desire to complete a doctorate in psychology. He asked me if I would consider hiring him part time and supervise him while he worked as a psychological assistant and completed his studies. Because of my own background of struggle paying for my college education, I was willing to help. His background of working with the poor led me to believe he shared my values. One day as I was preparing to take a specialty examination in clinical hypnosis, I went to see my former psychology advisor, who headed the psychology department. The professor must have been having a bad day. He was the one who told me he did not want me to practice psychology because I had not taken all my course work in *his* department. I needed him to sign the statement that verified I had taken particular courses. Since I had done so, he had no choice but to verify that I had, but he turned on me with angry venom such that I had not experienced from anyone before. I was shaken up by this and shared the experience with Darrell upon returning to the office. Darrell was sympathetic. He expressed the anger I was unable to express and told me the professor had a serious problem dealing with intelligent and successful women. Little did I know then his statement was a projection of his own feelings.

As the patient load increased, Darrell told me he would like to resign as director of the inner-city agency. He said he thought I could use his management skills and public relations talents to build my practice into the clinic I had envisioned. He believed he could continue seeing patients part time and manage the business ends of the practice part time. This would relieve me of time to increase my patient load. He convinced me, by pointing out the successful teamwork we had already demonstrated in a couple of projects, that it would not take long to have enough patients to more than pay his salary full time. I agreed; he began working full time. Things seemed to be going in a positive direction for a few months. Darrell was an intelligent man who picked up on my insecurities of being a woman in a male-dominated business world. (The opening chapter of *The Dance of Anger* [1985] by Harriet Lerner of the Menninger Clinic in Topeka, Kansas, addresses this quite well.) He also recognized I had what he called the "fatal flaw of a Christian upbringing in the modern world." I did not know at the time that he considered Catholic upbringing to be a fatal flaw. I truly believed, if I treated others as I wanted to be treated, they would treat me kindly in return. More importantly, I retained my belief in living my Catholic faith as much as I was able.

To further meet patient needs, I pulled together the skills of other professionals so more people could be helped appropriately. Developing mutual respect among colleagues and other professionals was fulfilling along with giving me many referral sources. My life was enriched by my vocation in many ways. Because I had done well as far as income and increased patient load were concerned during the initial four years of my solo private practice, my attorney and my accountant suggested that incorporating the practice would be advantageous as more staff were needed and being hired. Darrell especially encouraged it, promising to work harder on his doctorate so that he soon could be an integral part of the practice upon being licensed. While incorporations have advantages of structure with which to ensure taxes are paid periodically and regularly, the costs of being a small business employer were unbelievable. Even more than financial costs were the beliefs of much of the public and some employees. For example, there are common misconceptions only rich people are incorporated and a title of doctor brings huge amounts of money all by itself. Many do not understand or consider overhead costs. Moreover, because it was a professional corporation, I was the only shareholder in it; I could offer few incentives to people to work for building up the corporation other than profit sharing, health benefits, and paid vacations (which I did). Persons not licensed, who worked for me while I provided supervision, could not be paid on commission or percentage. If I hired anyone full time, the responsibility for paying his or her salary, until their caseload was built, rested solely upon me as did the administration of many legal and financial responsibilities of being an employer.

I hoped I could build a successful clinic without touching the savings I had put aside for retirement. I thought I could do this by not taking my salary for a few years and putting it into the building funds. Then, when the clinic became profitable, it would be paid back. Darrell convinced me this was a good plan. He said he regretted he was not in a position to take a cut in salary because he was the major breadwinner in his marriage even though his wife was employed full time. He was very convincing, emphasizing that I would be paid back with interest, so I should look at it as an investment; I did not recognize the inconsistencies in his statements. He reminded me both of us saw a need for such a clinic, wherein several specialties could work side by side with a holistic team approach. A team approach was designed to put a patient's best interests forward rather than letting the first priority be the furthering of one person's professional career. My husband began to question Darrell's motivations, but he also wanted to allow me to handle the practice on my own. His only condition had been to ensure home and office be separated to protect what we had worked so hard to obtain for ourselves and our children. Darrell became aware of his questions and cunningly told me he was sure my husband would prefer me to stay in a sole practice because "most men were threatened by wives' successes." I knew this was not true for my husband as he was supportive and encouraging of my work.

I did not allow myself to see beyond Darrell's charm and enthusiasm, which covered up his manipulativeness, opportunism, and greed. He eventually convinced me to borrow most of my savings (again assuring me I would get it back with interest) and go into debt two hundred thousand dollars more in order to expand the offices we occupied, to purchase equipment, and to educate him in biofeedback techniques. Later on, when trouble emerged, Darrell used the trouble as the excuse to leave, and I was incredibly saddled with all the debts. Even so, I still found it difficult to believe he was part of the plan to put me out of practice. I had to face the fact I never wanted to believe it and so used denial with regard to his motivations. As time went on, I learned more about his background. I soon realized Darrell had many emotional problems of his own, which, again, I would not allow myself to recognize. These were exacerbated by his fourth divorce. His unresolved anger over childhood neglect and ridicule, while growing up in a dysfunctional home, was directed at capable women. This was the reason he had recognized the professor's problem. He may have attempted to destroy the demon within himself by using and abusing women. Regardless, his influence fueled the fires. Hiring him was a devastating error on my part; I doubt I would have been the subject of a travesty of justice had he not been there. I gullibly allowed my better judgment to be ignored as my own pride became inflated with the dream of a successful clinic. Moreover, in spite of his shortcomings, Darrell seemed to be a very good therapist. By admiring the skills he had to correctly diagnose problems of patients, I doubted my uneasiness about his motivations.

Although the first year the clinic barely managed to remain solvent, the following year it fared better. We gained an excellent reputation, Darrell continued to spend the corporation monies because, he said, one needs to spend money to make money, and I, of course, believed him. Since he had an administration degree, I deluded myself into trusting he knew best about business decisions. By this time, I had lost confidence in my business skills as he continued to accuse me of being too conservative. At any rate,

Darrell wrote grants and proposals to attempt to obtain contracts for Employee Assistance Programs (EAPs) and other such programs. He hired persons to fill the jobs these were to create. Meanwhile, the health industry began to experience a trend in another direction, forcing private practitioners and clinics to go out of business. Health Maintenance Organizations (HMOs) and Preferred Provider Organizations (PPOs) were coming into existence; this resulted in increased health care dollars being used for hospital technology and decreased provider reimbursements. Patients had less choice about the providers they could see; many were forced to change physicians and other providers when their insurance plans were altered. The public seemed paralyzed to stop the trend as a health care crisis became apparent. It was illogical, but large sums of money were being spent on building outpatient surgery units, duplication of very expensive diagnostic machines, and health insurance facilities at the same time as money spent on patients' health care, especially mental health care, was declining. Whenever I expressed my concerns, Darrell told me I worried too much and I was attempting to make him feel guilty for spending money. I was not; I was questioning the wisdom of investing my savings and going into debt with loans that were getting harder to repay. Again, in retrospect, I know I was being the proverbial peacemaker, afraid of his angry outbursts, and doubting my own better judgment as I permitted his anger to control my decisions. Not having a crystal ball, I had no idea the price I would someday pay for my lack of assertiveness as I allowed him to continually diminish my self-esteem.

The trends, at that time in the health care industry, generated an envious competitiveness among providers. Instead of using team approaches or sharing ideas that worked, some projected their frustrations on colleagues, much as siblings do. For example, a female psychiatrist on one hospital staff appeared to look for ways to discredit or belittle me. A descriptive experience of this happened when a friend of our family was hospitalized in the psychiatric unit. My mother, knowing I sometimes had patients in the unit, innocently encouraged me to make a supportive visit. I was on the floor a couple of days later, so I stopped in. Asked if I could stop in again, but not remembering my home phone number, without thinking, I took out my card and wrote my number on it. Perhaps the psychiatrist just happened to see the card. I do not know. I only know the psychiatrist, at a staff meeting the following week, angrily, in front of several peers, accused me of trying to steal her patient. She wrote up a grievance against me to put into my personnel file. Her accusation was not only false, it was ridiculous. Others called it humorous.

Employees all over were demanding more benefits, oblivious to the problems of their employers in the eighties. This was especially true in outpatient mental health facilities as paperwork to get sessions authorized and then to file claims increased and more supportive staff were required. These trends began to cripple our clinic as time went on, too. It seemed that few were willing to take a few minutes to examine the expense side of the journal; they looked only at the income column. Simple mathematics, which they easily could have used, would have pointed to reality. All income was derived from patient services. There were only so many patient hours in a month. Liability, property, and health insurances as well as mortgages, loans, salaries, taxes, and other costs of running a professional office were increasing while the number of patients being seen was decreasing. Even so, had there been no expenses, profits were not possible to obtain with the income we were getting; but, if all worked together, all could make a reasonable salary and patients would receive quality care. The number of private practitioner offices and small service–type businesses which folded during the eighties was representative of increasing costs of employers compared to income generated by persons in service industries.

CHAPTER THREE

THE CRITICAL FIVE

————————※————————

*T*hings seemed to go well for the first four years I was in private practice, so my belief in others' fairness remained firm. I ascribed to the "just world" hypothesis, which suggests that, if you treat others fairly, they will treat you fairly in return. I now know this is not true in today's society for everyone. I realize this belief was a factor that opened me up to be used by others who wanted to take whatever they could from those who had worked for success without working for it themselves. As time went on and the nightmare descended upon me, I questioned my foolishness and stupidity as I was forced to realize I had ultimately been responsible for hiring the people who had conspired to destroy me even before they were hired. This was true even though I had delegated the responsibility for selecting prospective employees to Darrell, because I had not acknowledged he had no one's but his own interests in mind.

My patient load had increased; patients who had been referred were being put on a waiting list; I was uncomfortable with this as I wanted to help people when they wanted to be helped; but I had promised myself and my family I would not work more than sixty hours a week unless convinced it actually was necessary. Because of my conviction people cared as I did, I hired a psychology intern with a background in administration and whom I thought shared most of my ethical and moral values. Although I believed Darrell intended to help me build my practice, I now know he saw an opportunity to obtain his education without working or paying for it himself. Regardless, as he started to experience personal difficulties in what (I learned after he was hired) was his fourth (or sixth) marriage, his health began to suffer as well. Shortly after he was hired, Darrell required heart by-pass surgery. He acknowledged alcohol, nicotine, and other unhealthy habits had contributed to his coronary problems, and he stated he was determined to change those behaviors. As far as knew, he had not been drinking since I met him; I never smelled alcohol or thought he was inebriated. Thus, it never occurred to me to question his statements that his current ill health was a temporary setback. His debts increased because his wife required frequent hospitalizations for emotional problems. He convinced me he really needed help and would repay me as soon as he was able to do so. He borrowed money from the corporation and then did not begin to pay back the loan as planned.

I have no idea what he told his wife; however, when they divorced, she stated her attorney advised and urged her to investigate the corporation's assets. She implied the corporation had hidden some of her husband's money so she could not get it. While her assumption that he had hidden money from her may have been correct, the corporation's assets were not involved. She apparently shared her untrue allegations with Selma, the office manager at the time of her and Darrell's divorce. The cost of proving the allegations was not only financial. The employee morale also suffered as Selma and Lee (a therapist selected by Darrell) shared this with other employees. Soon, their behaviors became more arrogant and abrasive. Several years later, Darrell's ex-wife contacted me, and I realized how emotionally ill she had become during their marriage. Darrell had misled many people with his charm and manipulations. He was adept in using weaknesses and vulnerabilities of others to his advantage. At any rate, her divorce attorney had played right into his hand. By alienating her and pitting her against me, he had been able to legally steal thousands of dollars from her, me, and the corporation. At the end of our conversation, I assured her that I had no hard feelings against her and I was grateful she had contacted me.

Darrell continued to stretch the time line when he would be licensed and could become a corporation shareholder into an undetermined future. Meanwhile, I, as the only shareholder, was carrying his load and paying him to do little. He had appealed to and received my sympathy for his plight such that I became reluctant to ask him to leave. His illness and inability to carry his load was a financial drain on the corporation and me. When he realized he could not get any more money from me or the corporation because there was no more, he left. All financial burdens, for the additional investments and improvements he had convinced me were necessary, now were imposed solely on me. I learned that he had been asked to leave his former job because he had used monies there for his own benefit in much the same way he had with the clinic.

Meanwhile, because with Darrell's encouragement, we had developed the clinic concept (which I saw as an opportunity to help more people more cost-effectively), and we hired three others with specific skills to add to efficiency of the clinic. The first was Jazelle, hired to manage the business office. I had had an excellent and talented office manager before Jazelle. Unfortunately, her husband was transferred to another state, and she had to be replaced. Marvin, who had worked with Jazelle before, told me she would be a good choice, as did Darrell. Within two weeks of hiring her, it became apparent she did not have the necessary skills to handle the position. She may have been aware of this because three days before her probationary period ended, she became angry and quit without warning. With 20-20 hindsight, I recalled two important events. One, Darrell and I had a conversation about telling her she needed to obtain additional skills, if she wanted to keep her position, before her probationary period ended. This conversation took place the day before I took a much-needed day off. Two, Darrell took the following day off; this was the day she quit. I now believe these were not coincidences.

Numerous unbilled services and errors in billing, resulting in considerable loss of reimbursements, were discovered when we tried to put business affairs back in order after Jazelle quit. To add insult to injury, she sued me, alleging she had been forced to quit when she had threatened to expose me to the Medicare Fraud

Unit if her demands were not met. I truly had no idea what she was talking about, and an internal investigation was done to determine the basis of her threat. Her claim, as I understood it, was that I was overcharging welfare patients. The internal audit indicated this was not possible; but, as a nuisance suit, the attorney advised me to settle her suit out of court. This would eliminate losses of time, income, and patient welfare. Now, I know this was a mistake; under ordinary circumstances it was the right thing to do, but we had no idea of her connection to Marvin. I later learned Jazelle previously had sued former employers in much the same way as she had sued me in order to make money without working for it. Even though it was morally wrong, nuisance suits have been promoted by our legal system. The costs of defending yourself, when someone lies, give unscrupulous persons an idea how to legally destroy someone. Such was the dice set for me by the lawsuits of Jazelle and Darrell's ex-wife.

Darrell hired Selma to replace Jazelle in April. She seemed capable and conscientious; however, she had difficulty with taking instructions (especially from another woman) and even more difficulty with taking any constructive criticism of her work. It was her first job outside the home since she married; when June came and the school year was over, her personality seemed to change. I excused this, believing it had something to do with leaving her children alone during the summer days. Patients would later describe her as cold, abrasive, and rude. As time went on, I saw her as unhappy, bitter, and resentful. She often made remarks about my good fortune, totally ignoring the sacrifices, hard work, and twenty years of school that had prepared me to become a private practitioner. Her negative nature increased during the time of Darrell's divorce.

Marvin, the social worker, who had been working part time for me since I first opened my practice, was hired full time when he lost his primary job. This was in June, six months after Jazelle quit. By chance, when attending a professional luncheon, one of Marvin's former co-workers warned me to be careful about him. According to this source, he had used information he had gained in the guise of friendship to discredit others. It was the uncovering of his disloyalty that contributed to Marvin's dismissal. Foolishly,

I defended him; I did not want to believe he was disloyal. Again, my naiveté would prove to be costly. So, since I thought he was a good therapist, he was hired as a psychology assistant to help carry therapy cases while Darrell was recovering from ill health, thereby allowing me to attend to administration tasks previously assigned to Darrell. I only can surmise what led to Marvin's disenchantment and vindictiveness. Recalling his former co-worker's allegations and, in addition, I thought he was disappointed he was not given a promotion to vice-president like Darrell. Darrell had been given the position primarily due to his administrative degree and because he supposedly planned to complete his doctorate, take state boards, be licensed, and obtain shares in the corporation. (As a professional corporation for delivering psychological services, only licensed psychologists could own shares.) Marvin had no plans to become a psychologist. Soon thereafter, Marvin resigned. The investment in his training was another considerable loss. He had obtained a full caseload only shortly before he left; thus, for the six months he worked full time, he did not see enough patients to cover his salary.

Granted, fraud had taken place in some patient service entities, and there were some Medicaid providers who bilked the system. Nonetheless, Medicaid providers were warned that the fraud squad could make your life miserable even when you were innocent. At workshops for learning proper billing procedures, office workers were encouraged to turn in their employers for investigation, thereby promoting false claims like the one I was subjected to endure. Selma was sent to such a workshop shortly after Marvin was hired full time, so he volunteered to answer the phone and greet patients the day Selma attended the workshop. It was a mistake to hire Marvin full time, a mistake to believe he had nothing to do with Jazelle's threats, but my greatest mistake was not to realize he had resigned in anger and jealousy giving him the motivation to destroy me by misplaced revenge. Instead, I preferred to believe he left because he found a job doing more what he enjoyed doing, primarily working with children rather than with families and adults.

Regardless, while he was still working at the clinic, he had volunteered to help Selma research Jazelle's claim of overcharging Medicaid patients. They reported to me they had discovered she had not taken the time to check the dates of service when she filed Medicaid forms. The forms were especially difficult to type, she often said she hated doing them (as did Selma), and she devised a shortcut. Her procedure was discovered when the dates on the forms were put on duplicate account cards and compared with patient account cards. If the patient was seen three or four times in a month, she would use three or four sequential weekly dates. Most of the time, this worked well because patients usually were seen the same day and time each week or month. However, instead of over-charging, she had been undercharging; and many evaluations and several visits, which she had not submitted for payment, had been written off as uncollectible. In fact, it was Marvin who pointed out, with so many services not billed, the corporation had lost a considerable amount of money. (It was the memory of his words that made the shock overwhelming when things came to a climax and I learned Marvin was involved in the attempts to destroy me.)

Upon receiving the papers concerning Jazelle's suit against me, I called the Medicaid office and told them what had been dis-covered. They checked and verified their records supported this. After a brief informal audit, the matter was dropped with a mutual change of dates with the Medicaid office. Although there was a substantial loss of income, I decided not to resubmit claims billed incorrectly. I was willing to accept the loss and lesser payments because the expense in time and effort to rebill seemed better spent going forward and generating new income rather than trying to recover income from past services rendered. It was during the investigation when I learned Marvin believed the original state-ment cards were destroyed and the duplicate cards placed in the patients' billing files. Apparently, he told Selma they had altered records, which may have bothered Selma; however, neither of them ever mentioned their concerns to me. I could have reassured them that I had put the duplicate cards in a safe place in case they were ever needed for proof of the discovery. I assumed they both were aware of the resolution. When this came up during the sub-sequent Medicaid investigation, I had all the materials to prove what had occurred, including the record of the telephone calls to the Medicaid office. The Medifraud unit dropped any questioning with regard to Jazelle's threats as far as I knew. Nothing was mentioned while I was questioned during the Grand Jury proceedings. Obviously, the Medifraud unit found no way to discredit me with it and recognized it would point out the ridiculousness of the subsequent charges. The Medifraud unit was not willing to risk this.

As Darrell's health and motivation to work seemed to return and the patient load continued to increase, the gap left by Marvin was more noticeable. So, Darrell looked for a therapist to replace Marvin. We especially were searching for someone who could work with children. This was the corporation's position when Lee was hired. She and Darrell began to spend time together; his explanation was that he was assisting her in understanding the philosophy of our organization. (As time went on, I realized she and Darrell encompassed the characteristics described by Peck in his book, *People of the Lie*.) Thus, began the *nightmare*, an experience I would not wish upon my worst enemy. Lee was fresh out of a master's program, she presented herself as having had more experience than she did; nonetheless, suffering from battle fatigue, I allowed myself to believe her and saw her as willing to learn. She appeared to have good diagnostic skills and to be able to relate to children who, for the most part, related to her in return. Although she had little formal training in this area, I hoped, with supervision and directed text reading about therapy with children, she could become a capable therapist and a valued employee. When a few parents registered complaints, I suggested we work as a team. In this way, I was able to discreetly monitor her skills as I joined her in some sessions. It was not long before I realized she did not have the abilities I was hoping she had. Her therapeutic skills and writing command of English left much to be desired. As it was, because of the time factor required to build a caseload and her poor therapeutic skills, Lee never saw enough patients to earn a fourth of her salary. It was my caseload that provided the income to pay the staff, and my caseload was maxed. As had been true since I hired Darrell, there were insufficient funds for me to take a salary.

After a few months, I was taken by surprise when Darrell maintained the stress since hiring Lee was greater than any he had ever known with an employee. He stated the subtle pressures of her dissatisfaction—she said she wanted a raise in salary—were obvious to him, and he was becoming more stressed each day (as was I). I learned much later that Darrell and Lee had become friends outside of work hours. As this relationship became strained, the tensions at work increased, but I rationalized some of Lee's dissatisfaction was based on her not having enough to do. As I looked back, many signs of trouble should have alerted me; however, I allowed myself to be taken in by Darrell's complaints. I did not recognize that he had begun to drink alcohol to excess. Because an ex-wife was an alcoholic (according to Darrell), his wife-to-be had accused him of being one, too, and had told him she would not marry him unless he stopped drinking. Again, with 20-20 hindsight, I realized what I had attributed to his being upset by the divorce were personality changes brought on by his ingesting too much alcohol. He began to project his anger on me indirectly and to verbally abuse me. My uncomfortableness with anger made this easy for him. Additionally, he would make remarks disguised in jest to undermine my position and to discount me in front of employees and patients. I eventually would pay a high price for blinding myself with regard to his behavior. One of the subtle statements he made occasionally, which probably fueled Selma's and Lee's beliefs that I had lots of money, was uncovered months later. When I opened a small satellite office closer to Darrell's home and the homes of a significant number of patients, Darrell was learning how to balance the day sheets for that office. He questioned the sum of the final column on the sheet, remarking that it did not agree with the accounts receivable. I realized he believed it represented additional money owed. He seemed reluctant to believe it actually had no meaning other than to assist in balancing each individual sheet. However, because it sometimes was a larger number, his remarks about it may have suggested to Selma it represented hidden money. Any accountant could have told her or Darrell how foolish, in reality, this belief was.

Selma, with little experience in a doctor's office, did not bother to check procedure codes, billing changes, and reimbursable services for Medicaid. As I would later learn, she used Jazelle's statements and the suit settlement as proof of my guilt when Lee first suggested her scheme. Moreover, as time went on, she had become more ill-tempered and sullener. Yet I was naïve enough to believe Selma knew patient welfare had been, was, and would be the clinic's (and my) primary concern. On the contrary (as I learned months later), they had little knowledge of how the corporation functioned, the overhead involved, and the additional stress to me, because of the lack of initiative on their parts to really help out. Selma and Lee continued to plot ways to hurt the corporation and me. They erroneously believed they were being denied the perks of a large company while ignoring the pluses of a small professional business. Several penalties for late payments of the mortgage, equipment loans, and tax deposits alerted me Selma deliberately was not taking payments to the bank on time. It became one more task for me to do to ensure this was done. The cash flow could not handle expenses plus penalties. Also, when I periodically examined the day sheets and realized several evaluations had been overlooked and not posted, Selma became angry when I asked her about them. She told me she knew about them and had planned on posting them. To avoid further passive-aggressive behaviors from Selma, I ceased confronting her oversights. Instead, I asked her to work on developing some new forms on the word processor, a task I knew she enjoyed. Ann (an employee who had been with me for several years) then took over posting accounts. When I examined accounts more critically after Selma's resignation, I noticed the more services and work done to increase possible income, the more she was adjusting off accounts she labeled uncollectible. Perhaps these were coincidences, but I think they were probable attempts to maintain a poor financial picture as she and Lee developed their plans and followed through on Darrell's suggestions. This was reinforced by the amount of supplies I found when we moved our offices into one suite; Selma was continuously ordering supplies. It was unlikely she forgot she had put them in the back of the supply cupboards; she consciously was ordering duplicate supplies to increase expenses.

Selma was responsible for billing and obtaining reimbursement for services rendered; yet she, like Jazelle, did not bother billing for special evaluations; this required looking up a procedure code to use other than the day-to-day codes they were familiar with. Selma complained she was having several difficulties billing Medicaid services, so she was paid extra to go to a workshop to learn these specific skills. Because Lee had few patients, when she asked if she, too, could take the workshop, I readily agreed. That way, she could help Selma with the billing if need be. Looking back, I wondered what her motivation really had been. The two of them were to return and share with the rest of the staff any information about procedural or reimbursable service changes of which we should be knowledgeable. It was during this workshop that Lee and Selma learned several claims had been billed incorrectly, but neither one said anything about this to me. Instead, they confided in another office worker who recalled this during the investigation. In addition to disliking typing Medicaid billing forms and to billing some claims incorrectly, Selma failed to bill for several sessions and most evaluations. She would become angry when reminded to make out the triplicates for patients as they came in. This was true even though it was pointed out in her evaluations that she invariably was forgetting to make out two or three triplicates each day.

Lee had been advised, when she was hired, that since the corporation was too small to have its own medical benefit plan, she would need to obtain an individual plan. However, the corporation would pay half the premium. Nonetheless, because of my own beliefs about ensuring my employees had good health care, I researched several insurance plans and found four that would cover a group of three to ten employees. The plans were presented to the employees, and one was agreed upon by them. So, as the end of her three months' probationary period neared, Lee was given health insurance benefits, which were effective as soon as she signed a year's contract. Two employees, who carried individual plans, were pleased because they would have better benefits than they did with the plans they had. In addition, all employees (including Selma) now had a life insurance plan as well. Selma responded angrily because she did not get an automatic pay raise; she was covered under her husband's plan and did not need health insurance. Lee's benefits continued to be paid during the time of the suit she filed against me, when she was fired, as well as several months thereafter, until she was eligible to receive benefits through the agency for which she began working.

After signing her contract, Lee's work began to deteriorate rapidly. She did not provide adequate services to patients; she came late and left early. She was given several warnings about her performance needing improvement or she would lose her job. Finally, after consulting with the corporate attorney, she was fired. She then threatened to expose Selma for her errors. Selma must have believed she would be in trouble; she quit, "turned me in" to the Medifraud office, and "cooperated" with Lee and the Medifraud prosecutor. The day after Selma quit, the nightmare began. Meanwhile, Marvin had kept in contact with Selma and Jazelle. They got together and polished their stories. It took over two years before the truth finally began to surface. By then, it seemed too late to clear my name. I had been an ideal target, one who would not fight back, because, by that time, I did not have the financial resources or the personality characteristics to stomach the abuses and corruptions of the legal system and, most importantly, I had vindictive and vengeful former employees who would lie to destroy me. As I was to discover, when reading about the investigations reported in *The Psychiatric News*, it served the Medifraud office much more to make an example of a vulnerable person than to investigate someone who really might be bilking the system. Most persons actually bilking the system would not hesitate to sue the Medifraud office, and they probably would have the resources to obtain the help of the legal system to fight back and win. As anyone caught up in court wheels knows, many times it is not whether the person is innocent or guilty that matters, it is a game of win or lose for the attorneys arguing the cases, as well as which side has enough funds to hire the most experienced attorneys and to fight long enough to win.

Lee must have known she would lose her job; I learned she had had several job interviews prior to being let go. She was hired by a nearby mental health clinic. Within three months, that clinic was undergoing a Medicaid investigation. Selma obtained a job in a hospital in September. The hospital soon was undergoing a similar investigation. Perhaps, but not likely, both investigations were coincidental. Several colleagues questioned whether or not Lee was an undercover plant, which certainly would explain her lack of therapeutic skills. Months later, another colleague, after asking me not to reveal his identity, told me that Selma had confessed to him the details of Selma's and Lee's plans. She told him she was so stressed by it she had become a "witch" and now felt badly about what had happened.

Meanwhile, I continued to see patients no one else at the clinic was trained to see and tried to keep on top of the business affairs as Darrell pulled less and less of his load. From the preceding October until February, when he went on medical leave, Darrell had dumped more and more personnel work on me. Maybe he was angry for being put on medical leave; but whatever his reasons were, he no longer supported or assisted me and began to formulate the plans to destroy me even more while protecting him. He convinced me he could help more if we opened a satellite office nearer his home. At the time, not only did it seem logical, but I must admit I welcomed the possibility I would not have to deal with his frequent mood swings and outbursts of anger. So, once again, I borrowed funds and opened a satellite office. As the investigation began and I became emotionally spent, another colleague, Sam, offered to help me. He agreed to supervise Darrell's work at the other office for which he would be paid. He indicated he would honor the arrangements made with Darrell regarding the office so that Darrell's loans and education expenses would be repaid. This was not true. He also was an opportunist and was all too happy to pretend to help. He was not (as far as I know) part of the plan to destroy me deliberately. Instead, he saw the chance to capitalize on an unfortunate circumstance while relieving me of some burdensome tasks. I was grateful for this part of it.

It added to my pain, though, when Sam decided to take advantage of my situation by taking over the satellite office as his own. He then hired Darrell and ignored my pleas to honor Darrell's agreement with me. Attempts to discuss the situation with him were fruitless. I recall one meeting we had. I had asked my attorney to mediate the legality of his actions. The attorney suggested I attempt talking with Sam and Darrell first, hoping they would be reasonable. The meeting was a disaster. I still was suffering from the initial shock and pain of being victimized by the Medifraud office and being betrayed by former employees so I was unable to present my concerns assertively. Both Sam and Darrell remained arrogant and talked about superficial things rather than discussing the issues for which we were meeting. Knowing I was financially drained, Sam knew I could not afford to sue him for not purchasing the office or reimbursing me for the cost of opening it. When I reported my failure to my attorney, he pointed out the cost of any suit to recover what was rightfully mine would be more than the monies I was trying to regain. He agreed Sam was an opportunist and could use the Medifraud situation to get an out-of-court settlement. He could, by using legal maneuvers, prolong the suit to the point wherein the costs, emotionally, financially, and professionally, would be prohibitive. Because Sam was a colleague, that he took advantage of the situation was almost as painful and devastating as the false accusations that had been made to destroy me.

Sam confessed years later he had been taken in by Darrell's manipulative abilities. Darrell had convinced Sam that I had taken advantage of him, invented the negative stories about him, and inflated the amount of his loan and education expenses. It did not take long before Sam learned the truth. Because Sam also had another fulltime position, Darrell had suggested he could manage the satellite office full time so that it would make a lucrative business for both of them. History began to repeat itself. This time, instead of me, Sam was losing money. He had been assured by Darrell that, if Sam would pay him enough, he would make it worth Sam's investment. By the time Sam realized that I had tried to warn him of Darrell's destructive abilities, it was too late to pull out of any agreements made to Darrell and to me. Sadly, to Sam's mounting stress and enlightenment, Darrell's own psychological problems had increased. Sam, not wanting to face how much he had been taken in by Darrell, was reluctant to recognize them. Darrell eventually crossed the ethical lines with one of his patients outside the office. She filed charges. Darrell was brought to trial, convicted, and sent to prison. Sam, as his supervisor, faced malpractice charges; however, there was no way any supervisor could have known what took place outside the office, so the charges did not materialize. Nevertheless, Darrell had changed Sam's life, caused him much regret, and taught him the far-reaching consequences of evil in the world. Notwithstanding Sam's initial betrayal of me, I understood what had happened. After all, I, too, had been taken in by Darrell's clever manipulations. Thus, the rift between Sam and I healed with time, and I could easily forgive him and empathize with his plight.

CHAPTER FOUR

THE DICE IS SET

————————✳————————

*D*uring the 1980s, managed health plans grew by leaps and bounds in various areas of the country. Most of the plans advertised they were interested in decreasing the cost of health care. This made them desirable to most people who had become aware that health care was becoming affordable only to those whose employers had benefit packages, were on subsidized programs, or who were in the upper income brackets. The health care crisis was on the rise. Insurance companies and politicians were suggesting that physicians and other health care providers were overpaid. In reality, when compared with presidents of universities, CEOs of major companies, attorneys, athletes, or politicians, the majority of private practitioners, physicians, and other health care providers were underpaid! The cost of schooling, business overhead, office equipment, employees, liability and malpractice insurances, unpaid accounts, and collection costs were seldom considered.

Mental health practitioners, especially, were struggling to balance the costs of private practice. The public, as well as the administrators of insurance companies, were under the impression that emotional problems were caused by poor decisions of people and could be controlled by better choices. This may be true for some problems but is definitely not true for mental illnesses. The brain is an organ just as the heart, kidney, lungs, etc., are. In reality, the brain is the most complex organ of the body. Thus, there are many pathways in the brain that can affect emotional issues. In fact, the numerous causes for mental illness include heredity, birth traumas, environment, physical and mental abuse, and accidents, to name a few. None of these are the fault of the person suffering from a chronic mental health disease. Already, fees charged barely covered the overhead needed to provide mental health services for people, yet these health plans contracted for less than the usual and customary fees. The one good aspect of the health plans was a reduction in unpaid accounts if co-pays were collected at the time of service. However, few plans covered therapy for chronic type cases in which our clinic at that time specialized. Many managed health plans indicated to their subscribers they paid for mental health services; this was not exactly true because they often did not cover pre-existing conditions, mental illnesses, or intensive therapy for many of the emotional difficulties that patients might want assistance in overcoming for good. Providers were encouraged to render adjustment-type counseling or "quick fixes." For example, one could not attempt to cure an anorexic or substance abuser in eight to twelve sessions; these required frequent periodic checks on progress. Numerous hospital stays should not be recommended or needed when long-term intensive outpatient therapy was the treatment of choice. Hospital stays were much more expensive than long-term outpatient care, but many health plans, for some reason, were more concerned about cutting outpatient costs.

This was the battle that patients and providers faced. If a provider consistently asked for more than eight or twelve sessions, those sessions might not be authorized for payment or the provider might not have their contract renewed at the end of the contract year. Some plans required a substantial financial investment by the provider. Our clinic was not treating sufficient patients covered by such plans to warrant the investments. In addition to not having our provider status renewed on one such plan, we lost a major contract one month after hiring Lee. The financial drain of paying Darrell's and Lee's salaries when they did not have sufficient patients to cover their salaries was so drastic that I still had not received a paycheck for some time. Yet I usually was working about ninety hours a week and seeing an average of thirty patients a week in an effort to keep the clinic open and to avoid losing personnel. Darrell said he was not ready to take more patients and, when I tried to transfer some to Lee, the patients objected that she was not helping them. They returned for treatment with the stipulation they would not be seeing her. Her lack of therapeutic skills became more apparent with time. She was trained as a social worker and was excellent with patients who needed specific short-term assistance, but we did not receive many referrals suitable for this. Because of careful previous planning, however, the bills were paid, and the corporation remained solvent. I firmly believed we would weather the storm and become as productive as we had been before hiring Marvin. Before he became incapacitated, Darrell and I had begun to work toward obtaining several contracts that would provide referrals and would coincide with the corporation's philosophy. We obtained two such contracts that were interested in quality mental health care and could provide sufficient referrals to fill our caseloads. Satisfied prior patients continued to refer many new patients to us.

Thus, in November, with June as the target date, the future looked promising. In December, when Lee was to sign her year's contract, she took it home to look it over after Darrell, then the personnel director, signed it. She came in the next day with it signed. Then she stated she had wanted to be sure she could break it if she needed to do so. After she was fired, I learned she had taken a job at less pay than she had made while working for us and for which she had applied the week before signing her contract with us. She said she planned to look for work that paid more but would stay if we paid her more. This was impossible for many reasons. Her caseload was so small it was not covering even half of her salary, she was already making more than most inexperienced master-level therapists, and the quality of her work was so poor that she was not worth what she was being paid. Further, because of the poor quality of her work, I was reluctant to assign many new patients to her. She was unable to provide therapy other than crisis intervention, which was not the service needed by most patients who came to us. In addition, income for the corporation was down further than it ever had been. (Recall: I was not drawing a salary, and several services were not being billed.) Nonetheless, I remained confident things would turn around. But from that point in time, Lee became an uncooperative employee.

Perhaps Lee was a plant. There were several indicators that she was. Regardless, the clinic began to have more financial trouble as Lee became more uncooperative. She seemed unable or unwilling to respond to patients requiring more than crisis intervention; thus, she could not keep patients in therapy. She spent her time keeping the office manager, Selma, from doing her job. Selma was to submit insurance forms and, in general, to collect the fees for the services rendered. She had been sent to seminars on the subject, but collections continued to decrease. The reasons included a lack of follow-up, insurance claims not being submitted correctly or on time or at all, and holdups by Medicaid and other third-party payers. More and more of the accounts were being written off as uncollectible or sent to our collection lawyer, so we were receiving only a small portion of what was owed to us. Darrell and I had several discussions about the matter. He stated he was puzzled by the strange behaviors of both Selma and Lee as time went on. He said he wondered if they had enough to do. I never suspected he played an important role in what they were planning.

Lack of work was not the issue for either one. Selma had sufficient work to keep her busy, and Lee was asked to work on several projects until she had obtained a full-time caseload of twenty to thirty patients weekly. The projects would have acquainted her with the philosophy and workings of the clinic and would have been important contributions to all of us. However, any project assigned to her was poorly completed. In fact, for one such project, she was asked to proofread a MMPI interpretive book (which I had had a part in creating). Selma was placing the material in our word processor. When completed, it would shorten the required time of report writing as well as enhance the professional quality of report writing. The number of errors in the completed project suggested she had not proofread it at all. This quality of work made assigning tasks to her more work for me than doing them myself. Working 50 to 60 hours at the office and 20 to 40 at home weekly, I desperately needed assistance from office personnel I could trust rather than additional stress from them on top of their uncooperativeness

35

while I worried about meeting expenses. Yet, even though collections were down and income was inadequate to meet monthly expenses, corporation taxes were increasing, and the federal tax deposits were to be put into the bank the day after payroll or a 10 percent penalty was assessed. Selma often did not get the deposits or mortgage checks to the bank on time, which resulted in several penalties. Finally, I took over these tasks because I knew we could not afford the penalties. I was not recognizing the co-dependent traits in me or the behaviors that allowed others to resent my position or to take advantage of my conscientiousness. One volunteer, who had worked as office manager for me until she was unable to commit to full-time work, because she became a caregiver for her husband, sometimes came by to assist Selma with billing problems. She recognized something was amiss and spoke to me about it. She offered to help me on Saturdays when Selma would not be there. I gratefully accepted her help. She was a lifesaver for me. She also began stopping by occasionally and boosted the morale of the rest of the staff, who were being affected by Selma's and Lee's behaviors. They were trusted employees, and their loyalty to me was appreciated very much. With her help and their continued efforts to do what they could to help out, things began to turn around for us.

The burden of extra work, stress, and feelings of hopelessness were taking its toll on me physically. I learned during this time I had a congenital heart murmur (which had not caused me problems before), premature ventricular contractions (PVCs), hypothyroidism, and borderline hypoglycemia. All of these problems worsened from December on. In addition, a Pap test came back suspicious, and I had a stage-one cancerous tumor removed the beginning of March. During the following year, I had two minor strokes and infections due to my lowered resistance, all necessitating time off work; I continued to work as much as I could at home and returned to work sooner than my physician thought advisable. Darrell, Lee, and Selma were aware of these difficulties. Instead of offering assistance as did other staff members and my former office manager, they made more demands on my time. Ann, our receptionist, and John, a psychological aide, volunteered to go on part-time after a staff meeting alerting the staff to possible cutbacks.

A colleague, who was looking for a full-time aide, hired each of them part-time, and the clinic continued to pay for their health care. Again, I was grateful for such loyalty to me. Other staff members made it clear they would help in whatever way they could; they also expressed support by verbalizing the conviction that, working together, we would emerge from the financial crunch by June.

I earlier mentioned the possibility of Lee being a plant. Her husband was on a scholarship in the clinical psychology program at the same university from where I graduated. Moreover, the university was associated with a teaching hospital and another local hospital. Four local hospitals and several psychiatrists and psychologists recognized the need for a specialty psychiatric hospital to serve long-term patients. Both hospitals associated with the university were against building a free-standing psychiatric hospital because they had available psychiatric beds. However, their programs did not meet the needs of many patients being referred to them, and their recidivism rate was high. I was among the group who supported the building of a psychiatric hospital; I had researched the reputation of one corporation bidding to build a facility in the area. I was impressed by what I learned. The recognitions that it specialized in caring for emotionally ill individuals and that other hospitals in the corporation enjoyed a low recidivism rate especially appealed to me. I know my active role in bringing the facility into our area did not make me popular with the university, with those two hospitals, or with psychiatrists not in favor of the facility being built. Neither Selma nor Lee agreed with my viewpoint, and many problems seemed to begin about the same time my involvement with the psychiatric corporation began.

As things worsened, in February, I discussed part-time work with Lee. She had announced her desire to get another job in December, the day she signed her year's contract. I became even more reluctant to assign new cases to her when, soon after the January staff meeting, she told me she had applied for a job at one of the mental health clinics and was waiting to hear from them. She began coming in late for work and leaving for home early at the end of her day. Thus, I encouraged her in early February, when I informed her she might have to go on part-time, to consider looking for another part-time position if she could not find a full-time one. When informed in late February she would be placed on part time in March until she had a full caseload, Lee said she would sue me if I did not keep her full time. This, as well as her lack of therapeutic skills, added so much to my distress that my physician expressed concern and suggested I find a way to cut down on stress or face a probable heart attack. I used all the skills I knew about the mind's healing powers on myself. These, the support of my family and friends, my faith, and maintaining a positive outlook, helped to get me through. My husband, who had retired early, came in to the office to lend a hand with some administrative tasks on a volunteer basis. In consultation with him and our corporation lawyer, the decision to fire Lee was made at the end of March.

A week later, Selma resigned. Although Selma had worked for the corporation less than two years and had earned three weeks' vacation with pay (which she had already taken), she demanded two more weeks of vacation as part of a month's notice and so would work just two weeks more. I accepted this because I knew her work would no longer be of any quality. I remained oblivious to the idea that Marvin, Lee, Selma, and Darrell had devised a plan to try to destroy the corporation and me. I still do not know exactly what motivated them. I learned, about two years later, the workshop Selma and Lee attended in November of 1987 had given them the details of how to do this. It took them less than four months to plant the "evidence" and to designate financial difficulties as the motive for the alleged fraud.

As 1988 unfolded, several disasters around the world were reported in the media, such as the earthquake in Armenia, the Midwestern draught, Hurricane Gilbert, and the crash of Pan American Flight 103. There was an increase in local murders, robberies, and untimely deaths by accident or terminal disease. As sad as I might be for the survivors, when I read such news items, I was constantly aware of an inner belief none of these traumas was as difficult, painful, and unnecessary as the one I was facing. A basis for this belief was the recognition that some who knew me, whom I trusted and had given a great deal, had stabbed me in the back. Knowing Selma as I did, I had to believe she would have convinced herself I deserved what happened and would have judged me according to her own value system. I recalled her statements about a relative working under the table, a friend doing what she had to do to get her money, and a right to be compensated for her pain from an accident by whatever method she could find. In addition, she had obtained two extra weeks' vacation pay and unemployment benefits (to which she was not entitled) when she resigned her job with me. Nonetheless, I was determined to retain a positive outlook and to retain the belief good would prevail. Although I continued to think most people were influenced by good, I had begun to recognize some were influenced by evil. However, the ethics that ruled my life allowed me, in time, to give up anger at those who initiated the farce against me. If they did not realize what they were doing, they must have been uncaring, and I wanted to be a caring person. If, on the other hand, they did not realize what they did, I would not want the burden they must have of knowing they had harmed the lives of so many with misplaced anger, envy, or resentment.

In August of 1990, we learned the stress had taken its toll on my husband when he was hospitalized for congestive heart failure and cardiomyopathy. One of the treatments for this condition is heart transplant. His condition was inoperable because he had sustained too much kidney and liver damage from the virus infection that had caused the congestive heart failure. It was suggested to the family that it was a matter of time, and he might not make it to Christmas. We enjoyed each other and remained positive about whatever time we had, eating healthily and limiting whatever stress we could; happily, he survived three more years. When he died, I lost my best friend and emotional support. His death, although extremely painful, paled in comparison to the horror we experienced through this travesty. I always hoped the truth would surface publicly before his death so we could rejoice together. It was not meant to be. We had been unaware of it as it happened but, while he was hospitalized, we pieced together his deteriorating condition over the past couple of years. His resistance was depleted by the continuous stress and a virus that evidently had hit his heart. In May of 1989, he apparently had suffered a heart attack. He had been working, as a consultant in his field of expertise throughout the investigation, to earn money to help meet our household expenses. He had gone to Denver. He thought his sluggishness and excessive fatigue were due to the change in altitude. He never took another consulting job after returning from Denver. He continued to be more fatigued and complained about not feeling well. I encouraged him to be checked out thoroughly. When he made an appointment with our physician, he was hospitalized immediately. One year later, I was hospitalized and again underwent major surgery, this time for uterine and ovarian cancer.

Several tests were completed during my husband's hospitalization. That he might not survive one particular test was a considerable risk, yet the cardiac team encouraged him to get it. It was needed for treatment planning; without it, death was certain, but with it, he could gain some extra time. We were advised to get all his affairs in order. We had updated our wills after my stroke; however, it was recommended we also have living wills and durable powers of attorney for health care drawn up. As I sat in the attorney's office once again, I wondered what else would happen to us before the nightmare was over. Although the stresses plagued both of us physically and accelerated Connie's death, the love between us was strengthened. The memories we built continue to sustain me. Nonetheless, even though I can honestly forgive them, I cannot condone the behaviors of those who perpetrated this crime against us. It was hard to believe good came out of it, but my faith continued to sustain me, and I came to recognize others had benefitted by what I had endured. I do know I became a stronger person because of it. The words of a psalm often came to mind. In it, the psalmist reminds us God can create good out of mortals' evils if we trust in Him.

CHAPTER FIVE

THE FRAUD SQUAD COMES

*T*he attorney (not trusting Lee) had suggested there be another employee present when my husband (who acted as the executive manager of the corporation while Darrell was on sick leave) fired Lee. He, like I, had no idea Selma, the office manager, was so disloyal. Thus, he asked her to come into his office with Lee when Lee finally arrived for work. (As had become usual, she was late.) When he told Lee her services were no longer needed, Lee threatened to go to the Medifraud office if he fired her. Neither of us, nor the attorney, believed the Medifraud office would be taken in by a fired employee. Yet, when Selma resigned, she asked my husband to accompany her to my office. She gave a month's notice after negotiating for it to be two weeks. She said her reason for resigning was her uncomfortableness in being asked to be present when Lee was terminated. She said it had put her in the middle, because Lee was her friend and she knew Lee actually planned to go to the Medifraud office as she had threatened to do.

Perhaps because her behavior seemed so strange to us, both my husband and I vividly recalled the ensuing conversation. Days later, the attorney also questioned her statements. I told Selma that, while it would be inconvenient and aggravating, since we had been so diligent in maintaining accurate and appropriate records, we had nothing to worry about. We had done nothing fraudulent. She said she thought she could have made some errors in billing. I assured her legitimate errors would not be a problem. She mentioned the difficulties in typing the Medicaid billing statements and the coding problems she had had. Again, I reminded her she had gone to a workshop each time something new was introduced and there usually was a grace period when new codes were being incorporated. I asked her if she were regularly using the new codes she had learned in October. She said she was not sure and then remarked, "It really is ridiculous what people are forced to do to get what they think they deserve." We both assumed she was referring to difficulties she said she had typing the Medicaid billing statements. She stated her mind was made up to resign the day Lee was fired when we made her so uncomfortable by humiliating Lee. Trusting her, I remained without suspicion of the conspiracy to try to destroy me.

Two weeks later, Selma left on a Friday. On Monday, I was served with a warrant from the Medicaid Fraud Office to look for evidence of unethical practices and fraud. Selma had signed the complaint dated before the day she resigned. My attorney later learned that Selma had accompanied Lee to the Medicaid Fraud Office on her lunch hour the day after Lee was fired. Cases she alleged represented fraud were carefully chosen, ones I was to learn she and Lee had prepared so as to demonstrate their claims. Two men in police uniform with jackets pulled back by their hands on their guns and two plain-clothes agents began to gather the "evidence." The media had been alerted that a doctor was going to be arrested for fraud; they were outside the office with cameras set up. The next few hours were chaos and began a nightmare still fresh in my mind. Staff was in shock, patients were ushered from my office, and one little boy was in hysterics. (Fortunately, one of the men had some empathy, and I was allowed to calm the boy.) Records were removed from my office; a call to my attorney did not change anything. I rapidly learned neither I nor my patients had any rights when it was a former employee who said an alleged crime had been committed. Nonetheless, I followed my attorney's advice to cooperate fully. Although I was never arrested, from the moment those four men walked into my office until the day I was cleared of wrongdoing years later, my freedom was curtailed as one who was guilty until proven innocent. It was not the other way around as I had been taught from youth and which I had naively believed.

The day following the Medifraud unit's visit, I received papers that Lee was suing me for breach of contract and charging me with causing her emotional stress. Two days later, the unemployment office awarded Lee and Selma unemployment benefits, which, of course, increased the corporation liabilities. The benefits were awarded because they supposedly had left an unethical corporation with an investigation pending. The character of Selma could be recognized in many of her previous behaviors, especially since she also did not reveal that two of the weeks she listed were her so-called paid vacation. Where was justice? In less than a week after being accused, I was being judged guilty even before the investigation was completed. The possibility disgruntled employees could be creating problems or could be lying for their own interests was never considered. And as I told some friends, conspiracy could kill me, and it would not be called murder, in spite of the fact death took place just the same, through the hands of vindictive employees with the help of the Medicaid Fraud Squad. Who could have imagined the prophecy in those words? Indeed, I know the travesty of justice contributed to my husband's death. Much precious time I could have shared with my Connie was taken from us; that pain will remain a constant reminder of an orchestrated crime. He was, as Bette Midler's song says, "the wind beneath my wings." Within days after being served with the warrant, my accountant and a colleague sent me copies of articles they had found about similar investigations. As I researched more, I found several other similar accounts and sent copies to my attorney. He also researched some of the cases and learned of other Medicaid investigations taking place nationally. Many were described as "relentless and malicious." It was evident Selma had delivered me into evil hands.

Selma always had been willful and determined to do things her way, but I had allowed myself to believe she was doing the work she was hired to do. In August, before she turned me in, she had an automobile accident during her lunch hour. She got so far behind in her work that, in September, Ann was hired part time to help her. In November, Selma decided to sue the other person's insurance company for damages, lost sick days, and a whiplash injury. Many telephone calls during work hours were made on her claim. (Note: she had lost no wages, because she had not taken any sick days; however, the corporation lost the full benefit of its employee.) Looking back, I should have seen the signs Darrell had hired three emotionally troubled or incompetent persons (Marvin, Selma, and Lee); they had been out to get whatever they could from others without concern of the cost to anyone else. I should have—I did not. At one point, when I still was not ready to believe she set out deliberately to hurt me, I gave Selma the benefit of doubt, I wondered if she (being aware of Lee's threats to contact Medicaid) knew an investigation would uncover her errors. To prevent having to take responsibility for her mistakes, she could have agreed to assist Lee and place responsibility on me. Ann quickly learned how to bill most third-party payers (including Medicaid) correctly. She was not afraid to ask questions and to obtain assistance from others. Soon things began to turn around only to be jeopardized again as the next step began: the investigation by the Board of Psychology. I had alerted them right away regarding what had occurred. It was apparent by now some losses would never be overcome. There were moments of despair knowing how much was taken from my family because of my desire to help others. The wounds were deep. I prayed daily for strength, guidance, and increased faith.

I had heard laws were biased against small businesses, yet I was surprised and shocked by the amount of unfairness I was to experience. The charge of alleged fraud continued to be processed without anyone from Medicaid talking to me. Unemployment benefits were awarded to Lee and Selma, who should not have been eligible, without anyone from the unemployment bureau talking to me either. I was expected to foot the bill for legal representation, however, even if no funds were available to me. By this time my savings had been depleted, and my husband had received no checks since he had retired early the previous year and was no longer able to work as a consultant because of his heart condition. I had received no money from the corporation since Darrell was hired, and everything I owned was mortgaged. Bankruptcy seemed inevitable. I was trying very hard not to be despaired. How could these people do everything they could to force my husband and I into poverty in the autumn of our lives? We thought neither of us would be able to earn a lucrative living again; we had worked hard all of our lives, had lived frugally so we could save money for when we could retire, and always had treated others fairly and well. I was especially hurt because I had worked so hard to get my education, to pass the boards to be a licensed psychologist, to open a private practice, and then to provide for others an opportunity to share my success. Now everything I had dreamed about was being taken from me. This was the United States, the land of opportunity, and not a totalitarian or socialist state. I knew I was innocent of the charges against me (although for ten months I was not apprised specifically of what those charges were); yet, I was being treated as guilty until I proved my innocence without any regard of the aftermath of being prosecuted though innocent.

Growing up, the word "slander" had ambivalent meaning to me. I could not understand how anyone could destroy another person's life in a way greater than murder. After all, I thought, if one had a good reputation and strong character, others would not believe lies about him or her. I thought most people would consider the source or at least question the validity of wrongful allegations. That this was not true and that, in fact, the opposite was truer was a desolating recognition. Few, when apprised of the situation, seemed unable to forego wondering what element of guilt I might have. This was my first experience with the "fundamental attribution error" I had studied in my psychology preparation. Now I knew people would believe one must have done something to be in such a position, thereby allowing themselves to continue to believe it could not happen to them. Death would have been easier for me or my family to tolerate than the helplessness caused by slander directed against me. Death would have been over and finally accepted as a natural state of events. The slander would leave its mark forever and never be accepted. Recognizing the signs of the emotional trauma of being victimized, I began talking with a few of my colleagues. I kept hoping the nightmare would soon be over, I would avoid permanent emotional harm, and most of all, the legal system would prove my innocence.

Several years later, after I gained some equilibrium in my life, one of my specialties became that of helping those suffering from post-traumatic stress. Since I had been victimized, my experience helped me to empathize with other victims even more than I previously could have. It allowed me to encourage them to try to overcome the abuses against them. Knowing I had experienced a similar plight, many saw me as an inspiration. This gave them the necessary strength to begin the healing process by a belief life might be worthwhile again. Once they began to heal, their courage re-inspired me to continue my work to help others. In addition, when I was the recipient of a nurse's, office worker's, or store clerk's courtesy and kindness, I informed their employer or supervisor whenever possible. It bolstered my belief in people as I experienced more people with positive than with negative qualities.

But having been victimized by those I had trusted; some scars were too deep and too painful to be healed completely. I could forgive those who had harmed me, but it was impossible to forget the nightmare of the experience. I did not want to be an employer for a while. Instead, I was my own secretary and office manager as well as a private practitioner and lecturer. This turned out to be an asset as time went on; many of my patients were well-known professionals who appreciated the added measure of confidentiality this represented. Ann continued as the receptionist and organizer of billing needs, and another former employee, who had remained loyal, helped with managing other office duties. I retained an accountant, billing company, maintenance people, and any needed temporary personnel on a consulting basis. The accountant, who also was a professional management advisor, monitored my expenses, billings, taxes, accounts receivable, and other such business matters. In this way, I was able to get out of debt and obtain some money for retirement.

Our legal system promotes suits, and anyone can sue someone. Whether they win or lose, the persons being sued are forced to spend large sums of money to defend themselves so that only attorneys come out ahead. This is true, regardless of the ethics, reputation, or the integrity of the attorneys involved. I know there are attorneys who are compassionate and not motivated by financial greed because my business attorney and defense attorney did their best to help me. I came to believe such attorneys are few and far between. Thus, any temptation to pursue my dreams again passed swiftly as I recalled what the legal system promoted—psychological death at the word of any vindictive, selfish, or mentally disturbed former employee; the risk simply was not worth it. I kept the private practice for about ten years after the nightmare; I believe I helped many people to overcome problems. The desire to retire early and enjoy some retirement years with my husband was no longer possible; however, I decided to close the practice and contracted with a nursing home company for about five years to ease into retirement at seventy.

After Connie's death in 1993, however, it became harder to continue with my work. He had shared my struggles and my accomplishments as I had his. My inspiration was gone. Each evening, before I left the office when he was alive, I would call to let him know I was on my way home. He excitedly would answer the phone with, "Is this my phone call?" We would communicate through our amateur radios on the trip home. These special rituals had kept us close in more ways than either of us had imagined. When he was gone, the lonely trip from office to home was difficult; in some ways, it was more difficult than coming home to an empty house. Having advised patients not to make major decisions for at least one or two years after being widowed, I now had to take my own advice. No one could have imagined how much I wanted to give up the practice then. Nonetheless, the pain of his loss in my life was not as horrendously painful as the betrayal had been; it was emptier.

CHAPTER SIX

THE AFTERMATH

---❋---

*I*n June it seemed the Medicaid suit began to slow down. I fruitlessly hoped they had begun to see it as the grudge suit it was. However, Lee and Selma had talked to the Medicaid office again. In the middle of July, another search warrant was written, and this time they apparently wanted the business shut down until the investigation was finished. Without a trial, they were determined to put me out of business. Day sheets, statement cards, triplicates, billing files, medical files, payment copies, and appointment books since hiring Selma were demanded. A handwriting expert was to check my handwriting to prove I had signed all the claims. Since I had said I had done so from the beginning, this did not seem the logical reason. In addition, they wanted my computers (including my home computer). The reason for these new developments was that Selma told them there were secret codes that would unlock how this fraudulent money had been obtained and disposed of. My attorney learned that the fraud squad was frustrated by not finding evidence of fraud, which was why they had called Selma to come in. She chose to bring Lee along to vouch for her claim. The court agreed with my attorney that it was unnecessary to take away my ability to earn a living unless it was proven I was guilty, so instead they shut down the office for a week and sent experts to the office to investigate the new claims. This invasion of privacy and Selma's paranoia were the last straws for me, and I became angry. Previously, I was depressed and running the risk of a heart attack. Now, whether I had a heart attack or not, I wanted complete vindication. If I lived in poverty the rest of my life, I decided then I would sell everything I owned to get the money to clear my name. Eventually, my attorney convinced me this might not be realistic because the cards still would be stacked against me. He reminded me how few win their cases when they fight any government bureaucracy. I also realized rapidly the legal costs to fight the false allegations were beyond the monies I could obtain, no matter how hard I tried. I had never felt so helpless or afraid. Ironically, this was all because I was "supposed" to have obtained less than $2000 illegally; hardly enough to solve the financial difficulties Selma and Lee alleged were motives. Meanwhile, I learned Selma had bragged to someone that Medicaid planned to close my office. Furthermore, she had brazenly called Ann more than once to inquire sweetly how things were going. Ann was furious and would just hang up on her.

As time went on after the first search warrant in April, several things began to surface that indicated Selma was not only incompetent and vengeful, but she may have been emotionally disturbed as well. Perhaps this was the reason Selma had been so afraid of what would be discovered about her. Many mistakes were uncovered as we searched for answers to the charges; all the mistakes seemingly were designed to decrease income and cause financial difficulties. (I prefer to believe Selma chose to take an easy way out of her inability to perform her duties correctly.) Examples: a printout of all monies received from Medicaid for the past two years was checked against a stack of rejections that we found in a bottom drawer under old supply catalogs. Over $20,000 had been rejected because of billing errors, and these claims had never been resubmitted. This represented more than 20 percent of Medicaid claims filed. (Note: reimbursement on Medicaid claims at that time was about a third of the actual charges filed.) If the percentage held across the board for all other insurance claims, then $80,000 of the other insurance claims were lost. This turned out to be a low estimate; the amounts Selma had adjusted off during her brief time with the corporation were almost twice this. No wonder the corporation lost money every month she was on the payroll! We had been working harder than we ever had, but not getting many payments for our work. From January through March, several other insurance claims had been marked to go to the patient rather than to the clinic. When claims were rejected or patients did not pay, the amount was adjusted off the books. The result of all this was financially crippling by July. Nonetheless, with the help of those who had remained loyal through all of this, including my husband Connie, Ann, and John, we gradually reorganized the office and consistently billed properly. Just as daylight seemed to be approaching in this terrible nightmarish blackness and some monies began to trickle in, the request for additional records, computers, and so on, came. There did not seem to be any way to emerge from the nightmare soon.

The expenses of this unwarranted investigation continued to accumulate. Not only was the attorney required to spend hours dealing with the travesty of it all, so were Connie and I. Because Connie was retired, he was able to help me, but I was unable to see as many patients as in the past, and I did not have another therapist to help out in any way. We wore out a Xerox machine with copying pertinent information so as to function (and a coffee pot that was in use day and night). Hundreds of file folders and reams of paper were needed. So, it went. To top it off, the Medicaid office retained a box of old statement cards and other records. Although these were for closed cases, the cards and records had information on them that was needed at times to locate files of persons whose case name was different than the names of the mental health agencies or other practitioners gave when former patients wanted to resume therapy or have their records forwarded somewhere. I was grateful these were returned eventually.

Over and over I was reminded of the lack of respect given to the personhood of a welfare patient as this mockery of justice continued to try to cripple me. In fact, one of the reasons I had elected to treat as many persons on welfare as I did was my belief they had the same rights to receive quality psychotherapy and to choose their therapist as those who could afford obtaining premium insurances. For the grace of God, I could have been in their shoes. I often reminded myself of all the blessings in life I had. I treated many who did not have coverage, even by Medicaid, for the visits they needed. Persons on welfare were allowed four visits a month, so if they needed three visits a week in the beginning of treatment or while seriously depressed (and in danger of suicidal thoughts), I saw them for three times a week or daily. Thousands of dollars were written off per my direction each month because of this. Meeting them weeks, months, or years later, I was more than compensated for it when someone would come up to me in a store or restaurant and tell me how much they appreciated it. They would update me on their current improved life and tell me it was because I believed in them and treated them as being worthwhile and important that they had been able to pull themselves out of poverty. Ironically (or coincidently), during the time the Medifraud unit had instigated their witch hunts, a new guideline was established. Private practitioners could not knowingly treat Medicaid patients free of charge. According to this new guideline, it was considered a method to avoid government regulations. Not once during the investigation was the sensitivity of the information in files considered by the Medifraud unit. I was too shocked and numb to feel energy from anger enough to benefit from it. Instead, I felt helpless, fearful, and disillusioned.

Perhaps the worse feeling was the aloneness. When I lost my beloved husband, the loss was horrible. Yet, because of those who continued to emotionally support me, it was not as painful as the aloneness felt during the nightmare of betrayal. Psychologists in the area were fearful of any adverse publicity, so some did avoid associating with me. I understood. This was due to the fundamental attribution error, the belief in guilt by association. While there were several physicians and a few psychiatrists, only two psychologists remained supportive and assured me they believed in my innocence, so I continued to be affirmed and encouraged. One physician said that AMA (the American Medical Association), unlike APA (the American Psychological Association), would back a member financially in a similar suit. My children, brought up to think justice would eventually prevail, believed everything would turn out fine. It hurt too much to talk about it; when I saw others hurt with me, I remained silent. Keeping my parents informed was difficult, knowing the pain it would cause them; yet I preferred they did not hear it from someone unmindful of their pain. The arrogant abuse of power of the Medicaid prosecutor was underestimated by many people who believed the truth would come out and it would be over soon. (It was somewhat gratifying when, about a year later, I learned this prosecutor lost his job when another provider sued him for abusing his power.)

There were few I could really talk to about my disbelief, shock, and hurt that anyone would want to do something this horrible to another person. It was even harder to realize that those doing it to me were people I had trusted to be good people and, in some cases, my friends. When I recognized signs of depression, I contacted a colleague. She gave needed support. My closest associate had problems of his own, was too caught up in his own concerns to be helpful, and (although I did not know it then) was an integral part of what went on. Another associate, who offered to help, gave the appearance of doing so initially, and them demonstrated his opportunistic intentions and found a way to take advantage of the situation. I recalled his offer to take over some of my work, the supervision of my associate, and the running of the branch office with the promise of returning these to me when I was able to practice full time again. I ignored his avoiding behaviors and did not allow myself to accept the fact that he never gave me the chance to talk about what was going on. Perhaps his plan was to take over so gradually, I would not realize what he was doing. I learned too late, even the written agreements I had with him or my former associate were not protected by a legal system that had become so corrupt only its members can earn a living without concern of huge legal bills. Only the loyalty of my patients and my reputation of providing successful treatment prevented the total dissolution of my practice.

My aloneness in fighting this battle was intensified by the response of the Board of Psychology to the letter Lee had sent them when she learned she would be fired. Although the letter made several false allegations that could easily have been checked, no one from the Board came to my office, spoke to me or to the other employees, or bothered to check records. Instead, the Board forwarded the letter to the Medicaid office because, in addition to allegations regarding profession ethics, Lee had claimed fraudulent Medicaid practices. Since Selma had also gone to the court, I was presumed guilty. No one seemed to acknowledge the correlations of these actions. It was unbelievable the Board members, appointed to be advocates for psychologists, were so apathetic to one of their professional community. That the Board did not see through Lee's actions amazed me, but that they did not check things out appalled me even more. This could have been done without alerting me of what was happening should it have been true and, when recognized as false, could have prevented the nightmare. Years later, I was asked to accept a position on the Board. After careful deliberation, I accepted. Then, when I was on the Board, I was gratified to present and see implemented a procedure to prevent this from happening to someone else. The Board became more of an advocate for its psychologists. Although there may have been a psychologist I would not have referred a patient to treat, I would not have wished this nightmare on my worst enemy. I believed, then and now, any human being deserves better treatment than I received.

As that first terrible summer ended, we were not nearer to a resolution of the problem than when it began. No one from the Medicaid office had yet talked to me, and I had not been informed what specifically I was supposed to have done. Our youngest son planned to be married in November; I was too depressed and battle-fatigued to adequately share in his happiness, especially when I learned the jury trial for Lee's breach of contract suit and the grand jury proceedings were scheduled to begin the week of his wedding. Then Lee suddenly withdrew her suit. The attorney speculated and I believed it was because she knew she had no chance of winning it, and it would hurt the Medifraud case when her lack of credibility was exposed. Even though what was happening to me was wrong, it was supported by government officials and the legal system. It was the result of jealousy, anger, and vengefulness, and it was condoned by the groupthink adage of the doctor is rich and her employee is a poor victim. The irony was the people responsible for what was happening to me had all earned more than I from the practice while

Selma was the office manager. Moreover, Selma had not wanted to work during the summer. Not only did she receive unemployment benefits for not working that summer, but she had also been rewarded for taking away the livelihood of several, for destroying the dreams of many, and for making up a story to cover her own incompetence. I thought of the huge amount of money being spent by Medicaid to investigate her false claims and the good it could have done if that money had been used to benefit Medicaid patients by helping them get off public assistance. Few people realized that welfare recipients were penalized by loss of benefits if they worked. This was true even if they could not afford benefits for families. At that time, public assistance only allowed them to exist and not to live comfortably, so most preferred to get jobs.

CHAPTER SEVEN

THE GRAND JURY MEETS

———————— ❋ ————————

*L*ee had abruptly dropped her suit in the fall when it seemed probable she would lose the suit, which would, in turn, weaken the state's alleged case against me. Nonetheless, it was because of the Medicaid fraud allegations the involved attorneys decided each claimant should pay their own attorney fees. The legal fees incurred for settling Lee's suit were minimal when compared to the losses amassed by the Medicaid case against me. (It would take years after it was over to pay off the debt.) Moreover, the continuous costs of defending me against the false allegations accumulated rapidly. Thus, even though Lee received no financial gain from her suit, it added to the miscarriage of justice. Not only did the corporation have to pay legal fees up to this point, but my innocence remained in question. Beyond this, the losses in referrals and patient hours persistently increased.

It began to be hard to trust that my attorney was really looking out for my interests. The recognition he was concerned with collecting money from me more than looking out for my best interests was apparent when he billed for his services regarding Lee's suit. He originally had estimated her suit would take more time than the ludicrous Medicaid investigation. The contingency fee, which was required before he would even take the case, was several thousand dollars more than the cost per hour he used to settle her case, while the defense costs of the Medicaid investigation continued to mount. Did he apply or transfer the balance to it? No. When he did not, my respect for attorney practices decreased considerably. It became harder for me to trust I would be treated fairly by the justice system if my own attorney had so little compassion or concern for his client. When he offered to help settle Connie's estate after he died, I went elsewhere. Remembering the settling of Lee's suit, I could not feel comfortable he would not take further advantage of my situation. In addition, I believed the stress of the travesty of justice had accelerated Connie's death and robbed us of significant retirement money as well as many opportunities for enjoyment and happy memories during my husband's last five years of life. Thus, having him involved with settling Connie's estate would have added to the burden of his death by reminding me of the constant pain Connie experienced as he stood helplessly by, unable to end the nightmare for me. I hope I conveyed to Connie how much I appreciated his support and loyalty throughout the nightmare. I doubt I could have endured it without his love and concern. I understood why a former colleague who was similarly betrayed by one of his supervisees and others who made the news during the 1980s and 1990s committed suicide during their investigations.

In November, when the grand jury met, it soon became evident they were meeting only as a formality. Not once did it seem the Medifraud prosecutor was looking for the truth. Instead, he seemed determined to present only the information which would suggest I was guilty. He questioned Lee, Marvin, and Darrell the first day. Lee, with the complete stoic nature of her personality, presented the evidence she had planted with full blame placed on me. Marvin feigned surprise regarding being subpoenaed even though my attorney knew for several weeks he had been called as a witness. He told the grand jury I had instructed him to tamper with records because I had overcharged Medicaid patients. Darrell, fearful Lee would implicate him, stated he had no knowledge of billing procedures and so was questioned only a few minutes. The professional management consultant and accountant maintained the accounts were in order and the audit had uncovered no patterns of deliberate overbilling, signs of inconsistency, or errors signifying intent to commit fraud. The prosecuting attorney stated that anyone not working in the office could not testify about billing errors. My husband was questioned just before I was. He brought in all the records showing the rejections and evidence of unbilled services. The prosecuting attorney dismissed his testimony as prejudiced in my favor. Thus, no one was sufficiently questioned to allow the truth to surface. Certainly, it would have if there had been someone present who ascribed to the premise I was innocent unless proven guilty.

My attorney, recognizing I was in shock and so might not be able to represent myself well, was reluctant to agree having me take the stand. He said he believed there was a minute possibility the grand jury would recognize my innocence over and above the prosecuting attorney's overzealous and misguided execution of his job. I was questioned the second day from early afternoon to late evening. Selma was in an adjoining room. The assistant prosecuting attorney continuously went from the grand jury room to the room where she was and reported back to the prosecuting attorney. Several jury members slept through much of the proceedings. Since my attorney was not permitted to be present during a grand jury proceeding, this prevented any cross examinations of witnesses and little presentation of the mass of evidence supporting my innocence. That evidence was literally ignored. Allegations and claims by the prosecuting attorney were listed and never questioned. Whenever the local prosecutor introduced a fact that did not support the fraud squad's position, it was called irrelevant. After hours of being examined and cross-examined, when I came out of the room, I overheard several persons associated with the court talking about the case. They said they would be relieved when this witch hunt was over because it made them ashamed to be even remotely involved with such a sham.

The prosecuting attorney badgered me so loudly, at one point my attorney, who was waiting outside the grand jury room, demanded a recess. He and the prosecuting attorney went into a room. Their loud angry voices could be heard in the hall. I heard my attorney tell the prosecutor he was filing charges to discredit the proceedings because they were being conducted illegally and without due process, they were designed to prejudice the grand jury, and he was out of line to badger a defendant as he was doing without a judge or defending attorney present. When the prosecuting attorney returned to continue his subdued questioning of me, he brought in a stack of billing statements; for almost an hour, he presented them one at a time, asking me to identify each one, to read the statement above my signature, and to verify it was my signature. The statement read,

"This is to certify that I have rendered or supervised the above medical services. I understand that payment and satisfaction of this claim will be from Federal and State funds, and that any false claims, statements or documents or concealments of a material fact, may be prosecuted under applicable Federal or State laws."

Forcing me to read this statement repeatedly was done only for effect; nonetheless, the grand jury heard me state I had signed a billing statement over and over. No one stopped this, and no one pointed out there was not an employer or doctor anywhere who could have memorized, let alone recognized, which dates each patient was seen two or three months before signing the billing statement for services rendered. All practitioners would depend on their billing persons to do this work as carefully and as accurately as they could. Moreover, such billing errors do not prove intentional fraud. It was claimed $2000.00 was supposedly billed in error. The errors were in having incorrect dates of services and the CPT code given for psychotherapy rather than psychological assessment. That services were properly rendered was never questioned and, in fact, it was acknowledged that they were. (Note: This prosecuting attorney was removed from office sometime after my case for inappropriate court conduct in several cases; however, it happened too late for my case.)

The day after I was questioned was Thanksgiving Day. Selma was scheduled to testify on Friday. She was given prior knowledge of every question she would be asked so she would have time to prepare her answers. The grand jury did not know this. They were tired and upset about having to return the day after a holiday. The prosecuting attorney said in my presence, as he recessed for Thanksgiving, it was too bad I was not more considerate of them. All I had to do was say I was guilty, and they could be spared. Although things had been so stacked against me, I and others thought he had behaved so ridiculously, the grand jury members would not be swayed by his allegations. In spite of efforts to force his views on them, too many facts were contradictory and questionable. Thus, none of us awaiting the decision expected anything but an acquittal and were shocked when an indictment was rendered. My attorney immediately filed a petition to investigate the proceedings and to reverse the decision. The proceedings eventually were ordered by the judge to be dismissed. The following day was my youngest son's wedding day; I was able to get through it, even though I was oblivious to the world around me. Because I did not want it to spoil his joy or put a damper on the festivities for anyone, I told no one of the unfair and inappropriate decision until Sunday.

The Monday after Thanksgiving began outwardly as usual. Shortly after the office opened, a local TV newscaster with his cameras and equipment videoed the entrance to the clinic and tried to get an interview with me. The demise of a local doctor was news. Hourly, on one radio station, the announcement of the indictment was given; each major segment of that local TV station's news program carried the video obtained in the morning, and the major local newspaper gave it front-page coverage. Even if it had been true, many people recognized it for what it was: a witch hunt; many told me the recommendation of the prosecutor that I be sentenced to eighteen months in jail for billing errors of $1910 was not even equitable. Soon, supportive phone calls and letters, far outnumbering the few crazy, negative, and unsupportive ones, began to pour in. Other than several anonymous mock congratulatory calls and letters, most people told me the indictment was a disgusting hoax and the persons behind it were cruel, sick, or stupid. So, in spite of the pain imposed by the notoriety and the ridiculousness of my plight, I was uplifted by the sympathies of so many. However, this was short-lived, or so it seemed. Months later, people I talked with assumed it was over. Those who had heard the case had been dropped thought it was because the motives of Lee had been recognized. Some had forgotten about it. Others decided to find a way to take advantage of my situation. For example, a few former patients who had not paid their bills used the indictment announcement as an excuse not to pay them. Three years later, when my financial situation remained bleak, and legal counsel advised me to turn over old accounts to the collection bureau, I continued to receive anonymous phone calls from a few people challenging my right to make a living. My prayers included a recognition that Jesus had suffered so much more for the sins of mankind, was innocent, and was allowing me to have a taste for what he experienced. Thus, I knew he understood the trial I was going through. Over and over again, my deep abiding faith as well as my beliefs that right would prevail, justice would be served, and true friends would stand by me got me through some difficult days.

When family members, friends, or colleagues would ask me how I maintained my emotional stability (which seemed an impossible task at times), I told them my faith in God sustained me. When any one of them expressed having difficulty maintaining their faith as they watched the injustices leveled against me, I would tell them it was my belief God allows bad things to happen to good people, and it was up to them and me to prevent this from taking our most precious assets from us. Otherwise, those who were betraying me would win twice. The epistles of St. Paul and the stories of Job as well as my morning and evening Divine Offices were faithfully read; at times, it was difficult, but I did not want to become bitter and vengeful. (Some of my favorite psalms and passages were put in a folder for me to read over whenever I needed them. They are identified in Appendix B.) Regardless of what had happened, it seemed that continuing the cycle of corruption by trying to "right one wrong with another wrong" was not something with which I could be comfortable. Yet I was being forced to work within a system I recognized was being corrupted by the abuse of power. My family and friends continued to support and believe in me, which was incredibly helpful. Nonetheless, they frequently expressed anger at a system that offered justice only to those who could afford it.

Because of my own recognition I had enabled my employees to take advantage of me, I began working on me in much the same way I could have asked a patient to do. I read books on caretaking and on the causes of repression of women in our society. When

I realized the oppression taking place because of the Medifraud experience, I fought against falling into the victimization syndrome (sometimes called post-traumatic stress disorder [PTSD], defined as an emotional disorder characterized by extreme anxiety following an overwhelming, traumatic event). I read several books on PTSD and on codependency. (Note: the definition of codependency to which I adhere comes from an article by Robert Subby in the book *Codependency, An Emerging Issue*: "An emotional, psychological, and behavioral condition that develops as a result of an individual's prolonged exposure to, and practice of, a set of rules—rules which prevent the open expression of feeling as well as the direct discussion of personal and interpersonal problems.") Through reading, prayer, and support of family and friends, emotional healing began. My physical health, however, was precarious. Knowing I might die, I prepared for that possibility by getting all my affairs in order and by selecting the celebrant, songs, and readings for my funeral Mass around the theme of peace. I included a letter to be read at the Mass, begging those who cared about me to pray for peace and not to hold grudges toward those responsible for my death. Each day, even now, I thank God for the gift of another day and for sparing my life for my family's sake during those nightmarish weeks, months, and years. My husband's life, however, was not spared. Connie, weakened by the stress and pain of watching me go through this travesty, was unable to fight the virus that caused his congestive heart failure. Less than five years later, he died, and I lost my best friend and supporter. The talks we had had about his impending death were the strengths that kept me from losing my own will to live even though I found the prospect of life without him bleak and empty.

Meanwhile, legal defense expenses mounted continuously. Going on to a trial where I was certain to be completely vindicated was becoming an idealistic wish. I simply could not afford to obtain the justice due me, and I was not eligible for a public defender unless I lost my home. The Fraud squad found many reasons to delay the process. Their strategy, according to my attorney, to wear me down physically, financially, and emotionally was bound to work in their favor. I was one person fighting an army.

Statements made to me by others included: "How much justice can you afford?" "Attorneys are not searching for truth; they are in a battle in a courtroom to win the verdict by delivering the most convincing rhetoric." "Law schools help attorneys learn to shade the truth with a straight face and a disarming countenance." "One can obtain justice, but the way is not with truth but with money." In spite of what I was being told, I wanted to believe not all lawyers fit these descriptions and truth would eventually prevail. Believing this, however, became harder and harder. My attorney did not seem to be working for me but for the system, yet others told me he was doing his best to fight a government organization. There was no way I could finance a full-jury trial. Even if I were eventually to win and the state then ordered to pay my legal expenses and to give me a settlement, receiving the settlement could take years. Meanwhile, I would have to supply the funds to defend myself. I continued to be guilty until proven innocent. Family, patients, and friends were suffering more than words can describe. My husband's health was affected negatively by the stress; he was more important to me than even my reputation, so I wanted to give up the fight. The thought of going to jail should I plead guilty was the one thing that prevented me from giving up because I knew I was innocent. Saying I was guilty just did not seem the right thing to do. Nonetheless, when the Judge ordered the grand jury to review the charges against me, the indictment was dismissed. (This news did not make the papers, of course, so many were unaware of it.) But the legal system demanded another grand jury investigation take place, so there was little joy in the announcement.

CHAPTER EIGHT

THE PLEA BARGAINING

———— ✳ ————

*T*he relentless abuse I had known during the previous investigation and grand-jury trial had taken its toll in many ways. The thought of going through another investigation was frightening, but I was more frightened of not doing so, since I had no idea what would happen if I gave in to the state's prosecuting attorney's demand to admit I was guilty of that I knew myself to be innocent. I hoped the new investigation would uncover the truth and eliminate the need for an indictment or trial. I had been experiencing occasional chest pain. One morning after the indictment had been dropped, I was awakened about midnight with pain and the realization that the right side of my body was numb. I tried to get out of bed by holding on to the table beside my bed, but I could not feel it nor could I feel my right leg or foot beneath me, and I fell to the floor. I somehow managed to return to bed. I prayed for death rather than paralysis. Morning came, and I cautiously alerted myself. My right side was still numb, but some feeling had returned. An examination determined I had had a light stroke. My physician said it was a warning and prescribed medication to regulate my heart. Family, friends, and attorney questioned the wisdom of continuing to fight a government organization because the legal process would take so much time. Yet, we all knew we were at the mercy of a prosecutor who would not care about my life and who was determined to win because his reputation was at stake and considerable money had been spent to prove the state's case. My reputation would be under suspicion during another investigation, and my attorney was certain they would find as many ways as possible to delay a trial just as they had before. Thus, I eventually could lose my home, my professional status, and my life before it was over.

The state's prosecuting attorney had presented my attorney with an alternate plan, which he said would save taxpayer money, court time, and my legal fees. It was a legal formality, I was told, one familiar to most attorneys as a way of settling the issue out of court and not an admission of guilt. He wanted me to plead guilty to lesser charges; his first proposal was totally unacceptable to me because it stated I was guilty of unintentional fraud. After several hours of the attorneys deliberating in a separate room, my attorney emerged with what he stated was the minimum charges that the prosecuting attorney would accept. He suggested I accept the proposal rather than to have my life in turmoil for another five or six years while the legal wheels turned slowly. However, it would not be the full vindication I wanted. I would appear before a judge for what was called a determination of plea bargaining based on new information warranting a grand jury investigation—the allegations of Selma and Lee. In essence, as I understood it, I would be agreeing Selma had incorrectly billed for services rendered. I would pay the State $1910 they alleged I had received illegally and would not bill for $9000 due me, which had not been billed correctly, and not hold the state responsible for wrongful prosecution. I had to state that I knew of their activities even though this was not true, in order to release the state from the duty to sue Selma and Lee for false charges. These admissions were misdemeanors rather than felonies, which the indictment had alleged were committed. Further, I would agree not to see welfare patients for a year. In one year, my record would be expunged because I had nothing on it, not even a traffic ticket. Most of all, the trauma was to be over, and I supposedly could get on with my life. Although, admitting I knew of Selma's actions, when I did not, posed a moral dilemma for me, I recognized I had been negligent in not monitoring her activities more closely. Since, like most practitioners, I had not understood the complex Medicaid billing system completely (which was frequently updated with changes to the codes); I had naively believed in Selma's integrity, assumed she would communicate any problems she was having, and thought sending her to workshops to learn the procedures would be an assurance she was billing Medicaid appropriately. (As a result of what happened to me and other providers, there have been modifications of that system, and practitioners have been alerted to what the system was allowing vindictive employees to do.) After much agonizing thought and prayer, with the advice and support of family, friends, and attorney, I accepted what I hoped would be the lesser of two evils. Nonetheless, as I stood before the judge that day in court, I did not feel good about what was happening to me. Frankly, the thought of giving up citizenship in a country whose legal system made such a travesty possible briefly crossed my mind. I reminded myself it was not my country that was responsible but some power-hungry people who were playing games with peoples' lives just for their gains.

Within a couple of weeks, I was surprised to receive a notice the Federal Medifraud investigation would begin. This was not according to what I thought the agreement had been. My attorney communicated with them, and he said they told him it was a formality and they *probably* would accept what the local courts had decided. I, as well as my attorney, had notified the Board of Psychology before accepting the plea bargain because I was prepared to go to a full-jury trial if my license to practice psychology was in jeopardy. The Board said they would begin their investigation as soon as they received the court's determination. It took six months more for the Board's investigation to be completed. It was then I began to realize that what was usual in the court system as a settlement out of court and not an admission of wrongfulness would not be understood outside the legal system the same way. Plea bargaining has become synonymous with pleading guilty to a lesser crime and thus receiving a lesser sentence. As I obtained more information about other cases throughout the United States and learned the prosecuting attorney had a quota of convictions to obtain (See Appendix A), I understood why the attorney for the Medifraud unit would not accept the "no contest" pleas. Those who had previously done so were able to have their cases reviewed and to win settlements for pain and suffering for wrongful prosecution. There was no way the state's prosecuting attorney wanted to risk that. His quota of convictions and his job would be in serious jeopardy if that happened.

The Board of Psychology, to aid in their investigation, received copies of my signed statements and the judge's determination from the Medicaid fraud unit; they did not get recordings of the actual proceedings or of the biased grand jury inquiries. Thus, they may have been placed in an awkward position. At any rate, the Board determined, because of the adverse publicity, they needed to issue some reprimand to me. They suspended my right to practice psychology for at least fifteen days. One Board member called me and said, "You can use a vacation after all this." A reprimand would be published in the Board's professional journal. As before, some of my colleagues used this to *try* to discredit me further with other professionals, who had in the past referred patients to me, and with the boards of the hospitals where I had adjunct privileges. One colleague, who purportedly had made statements suggesting other psychologists should support and assist me in this ordeal because it could have happened to any one of them, advised me of the replies to his statements. One stated there was no guarantee that, by standing together as a unit, psychologists could stop the abuse of Medicaid investigations. Another said it would be better if I left the profession; otherwise, the bad publicity could hurt them, and they had their reputations to consider. Still another said he hoped the Medifraud unit did not think he was my colleague because they could target him, too.

As the Board of Psychology's investigation was taking place, again, physician friends saw clearly what was happening and were supportive. The additional time lost in seeing patients, especially those who had been having difficulty going two weeks without an appointment, decreased patient load even further and put more strain on cash flow. Further, I had begun to receive rejections to renewing contracts, as they expired, to remain on providers' lists from several insurance companies, even those on which I had been a provider for years. The reason was discovered. The

Clearing Board of the insurance companies received a statement I had been convicted of the crime of fraudulent billing of Medicaid claims from the Medicaid office. Although my attorney drafted a letter of clarification, not all rescinded their decision to keep me off their providers' lists. Dissolving the corporation seemed inevitable as I had lost any desire to rebuild the clinic or to hire other employees; my losses had been overwhelming, and the expenses continued to be too high for one therapist to practice in a clinic designed with space and equipment for several mental health professionals. Unfortunately, the mortgage had become my responsibility. Because of the financial situation, I could not afford to sell the offices for less than what I owed on the mortgage; however, the real estate market was flooded with office space, so I thought it was unlikely it would be sold soon enough to prevent bankruptcy. I still resolved to avoid that if at all possible and somehow managed to accomplish that goal.

Shortly after the State Board had completed its investigation, I received a certified letter with a notice from the Ethics Committee of the American Psychological Association. Lee had written a letter to the Ohio Psychological Association's Ethics Committee when she purportedly learned the indictment was dropped. Upon obtaining the copies of the court statements and records, they had initiated an investigation of my ethical practices and forwarded her letter to the APA. I phoned my attorney: "I signed those papers under duress. Reopen the case. Enough is enough. I want a chance to prove my innocence even if I die doing it." I was convinced the results of the out-of-court plea bargain settlement, to which I had agreed, were costing much more physically, emotionally, financially, and professionally than any jury trial would cost me. At this point I could no longer consider Medicaid funds or taxpayers' money. Reading the August issue of *The Psychiatric Times*, I learned a Hawaiian psychologist recently had been awarded $600,000 in damages after a jury found he was a victim of malicious prosecution by the Hawaii Medicaid Fraud Unit. Since my case was so similar, I was certain I would have a better chance of fairness in the court than I currently was receiving at the hands of my professional peers. I also realized, knowing what I had already suffered, that even a settlement of $600,000 was pennies in comparison with what I knew that psychologist had suffered over the last five years. My attorney momentarily calmed me. Then he informed me the court would require that I fire him, find another attorney who would need to sue him for inadequately representing me, and win that suit before my case could be reopened. This was scarier to me than anyone can imagine. I had no trust in the legal system by this time, and I doubted another attorney would agree my attorney had inade-quately represented me; I knew he had done his best with all the circumstances handed to him. The costs would be prohibitive in my present financial state if I lost. Hence, I decided to wait it out. He would phone Lee and threaten to sue her for harassment if she continued her attempts to discredit me. Eventually, both national and state ethics committees sent me letters stating, although I may not have supervised my employees as well as I might have, neither recommended removing me from their respective organizations or have my license revoked. Even so, I felt as if I continued to have a stigma attached to my reputation and ethical practices.

The letter from the Board in January of 1990 advising me I had a right to a hearing only added to my distress. Upon completing their investigation in October of 1989, the State Board informally had advised my attorney they would require a fifteen-day sus-pension if I did not request a hearing. If I requested a hearing, I would either receive no suspension, a suspension of forty-five days to six months, or a revocation of my license. This was con-trary to what they had led my attorney and I to believe when we discussed the misdemeanor pleas. Now they were stating the need for a reprimand was due to having plea-bargained. Every time I turned around, I was hearing those words: "You did agree to plea bargain." My attorney suggested I talk to some of my supportive colleagues to learn their thoughts regarding my chances with the Board. Because of knowing the reputation of the former professor who was on the Board, most did not think I would receive fair treatment. He worked for one of the hospitals that had attempted to squelch my testimony for bringing in the free-standing psychiatric hospital. Moreover, Selma had started working for that hospital. So, with the cards stacked against receiving a fair hearing, colleagues and attorney advised me to take the suspension rather than causing more waves by fighting the Board. I took the advice; by this time, I should have known better. Yet, again, there is no telling how things would have worked out if I had not.

My attorney communicated to the Board by telephone I would accept the suspension. Then, the fifteen-day suspension was increased to twenty days. Supposedly, according to my attorney, it was due to the time and additional effort my considering the hearing had required of them. In addition, the former professor Board member gave a copy of the agreement to the hospital board on which he served before I even received an official notice from the Board and was able to notify the hospitals' medical boards myself. After notifying each of the five hospitals, where I had affiliate staff memberships, that the Board had temporarily suspended my license, I began to receive notices from four hospitals that my staff privileges were in danger of being terminated. An explanation to one was all that was needed to obtain reinstatement. From then on, when any of my patients needed hospitalization, I would refer them, if their insurance allowed it, to that hospital and to the one whose president sarcastically said he thought the reprimand was ridiculous. He noted my clinical skills had not been in question and few practitioners would have been able to recognize the minor billing errors made. He thought most of my colleagues have realized the situation was trumped up. Another hospital asked me to reapply and promptly reinstated my staff membership. A hearing before a medical staff committee was required by the third, after which I was reinstated, when my Board suspension was completed. However, the information I had been briefly suspended was used by the hospital's PPO to temporarily take me off the provider list. (This meant I could see a patient, but I would not be paid to do so.) The fourth hospital, the one which the Board member had given a copy of the agreement, required a hearing and a reapplication process. Nevertheless, I finally obtained reinstatement when the hospital's attorney examined the evidence and verified the investigation was intrusive, abusive, and excessive. He recommended (along with other medical hearing committee members) my clinical affiliate staff privileges be reinstated immediately. This, by the way,

69

was the same hospital where my cousin's psychiatrist had tried to abase me. Notwithstanding this, I continued to enjoy good relations with most of the persons on staff there as I still do today.

When I had researched the backgrounds and reputations of psychiatric hospitals, I began to consider working within such a hospital on a full-time basis. I believed, with my extensive preparation and expertise, I would have something to offer the patient population and be an asset to the staff. Further, I knew I would like working in that environment. I applied for a position on the staff of the hospital for which I testified and which eventually was built in our area. The administrator of the hospital knew the three professionals (including myself) had endured harassment from some of our peers, had lost status at other hospitals, and had been investigated by a few third-party payers, including Medicaid/Medicare. I was the only one, however, who had the misfortune of firing an employee who began a vindictive effort to destroy my livelihood. Nonetheless, I was surprised when my application was not considered, until I was told by the administrator of the hospital the former professor Board member and one of the psychologists who had fought against the hospital's coming to the area were inadvertently made members of the psychological advisory board. Although the administrator and two psychiatrists on staff attempted to block these two board members' unfavorable statements regarding my application, they were unsuccessful. Other members voiced concern the Medifraud suit could cause the hospital embarrassment down the road. One more obstacle had been thrown in my path by the very forces that had been partially responsible for initiating my problems with Medicaid. I thanked the administrator for his support and statement that I was his first choice to join the staff. A few years later, he asked if I was still interested in joining their staff; I declined because I had begun working for another organization and was happy with that choice.

By this time my financial state of affairs was so terrible, I obtained another job to pay the expenses and put my office up for sale. I continued to see patients on a part-time basis, who were willing and able to pay me directly for my services. My efforts eventually worked, and my financial situation was resolved. I had

sent out many resumes hoping to find work in my field of expertise. My age was against me (although this was not directly stated),
and my extensive background overqualified me for most available
positions. A few favorable initial responses cooled quickly when
the fact I had been investigated by Medicaid came up. Knowing I
was an excellent psychotherapist, I was determined to continue to
do what I was most suited to do even if I had few patients until the
light at the end of the tunnel could be seen. Many expressed their
hope I would be able to stay in practice. I was encouraged, though
saddened by the injustice, when someone from APA apprised me I
had remained in practice longer than most caught up in this abuse
of power. A few had serious physical problems develop and were
unable to continue full-time work. Some committed suicide to end
the ordeal for their families. Many had lost their homes, cars, and
marriages within the first two years as their livelihood was taken
away from them and the emotional trauma therein took its toll. It
did not matter if they were guilty or not guilty, the results were the
same. When being hurt so much, they wanted to forget the nightmares and quietly disappear. Their leaving the mental health profession and losing any motivation to continue to pursue justice for
them, as well as not having financial resources to obtain justice,
enabled the abuse to continue even more. Efforts to initiate suits
for restraint of trade, discrimination, or constitutional due process
violations were cautiously organized by some with the awareness
that any legal action taken would be a costly and lengthy procedure.
I was blessed and believe it was due to my faith that I survived.

CHAPTER NINE

THE SAGA CONTINUES

———————— ✳ ————————

*T*he so-called federal investigation took another year. When it was over, I received a sanction from Medicare/Medicaid. I could not treat any patient on a government-assisted program for another five years. This was part of Inspector General Kusserow's plan to ensure the doctors he sanctioned would no longer have the ability to earn a living through their chosen professions. I knew from what had happened to others that the notices sent to insurance carriers, hospitals, and clinics would probably make it impossible for me to remain on many provider lists, which, in turn, could make me a liability to most employers, hospitals, or clinics. I would be over sixty years by then and would have little likelihood of rebuilding a practice. I began to really understand the enormous ramifications of the decision to plea bargain and my attorney's failure to explain the possible consequences to me. It felt as if I had chosen to die slowly rather than quickly, and I thoroughly understood why other innocent practitioners had committed suicide. Was there any way out of this dilemma? I could not change that decision or the resulting consequences. By telling my story, I want to warn others of consequences I had no idea were a possibility. While I wished someone had warned me, I could not know if I would have heeded the warning. I do know I could not turn back nor could I know if selling my home and anything else of material value to pay for a jury trial would have made me feel better. There was no way to know if the stress, pain, or costs of winning my case at trial (as I was certain I could have eventually done) would have erased the memory of what had already taken place.

The twenty-day suspension of my license also had consequences as time went on. Although my legal record could be expunged, the record of it would, in fact, not be because of the Board of Psychology's action. Every time I had to fill out the reviews for hospital reapplications, liability insurance reapplications, or any other form dealing with my professional work from that time on, the question would stab my inner soul. I would be reminded of what had been done to me and be forced to relive the pain over and over. Had I even done the wrong I was accused of doing or intended to do that wrong, perhaps it would not have been so hard to face. If I thought I deserved some punishment, even though it would be excessive when compared to the crime committed, I could have endured that punishment more easily than the travesty of justice I was experiencing. What made this so painful was the knowledge I had not deserved it at all. I took solace in Christ's message that bad things happened to good people, and Job's strong faith remained an inspiration to me to remain strong, too. It gave new meaning to Christ's sacrifice for all people, especially since Selma and Lee had betrayed me during Easter time. The anniversary of my employees' betrayal of me became symbolic. I worked at accepting it to be the cross I was asked to carry in order to gain an eternal life of happiness after my death.

Ironically or coincidently, the Board's suspension took place in April two years after the betrayal. Eastertime in the northern hemisphere is also nature's season of the year that emerges from the winter's death and brings spring's renewal of life. I gained courage and hope from this symbolism of nature's cycle. I concentrated on focusing on the present and the future bringing new growth and energy rather than on the past's destructive forces. I also considered the symbolisms of rest and dormancy so as to let the creative part of my brain positively function. Nonetheless, the liturgical season was most felt. As a child, I had prayed to help Christ carry his cross, so now I often wondered if I would have the strength to follow through with His request of me should that be what this trial was all about.

As time went on, my Christian faith continued to sustain me. As I read my Office each day, prayed throughout the day, and participated in the celebrations of my faith, I felt closer to God than I ever had before. The biblical readings would at times seem to speak directly to me. I found much solace in the Book of Psalms. So many of the passages seemed to echo the words I cried out to God in my pain.

There were moments as I distributed the Eucharist, read the Scriptures at Mass, or lectured to groups when I recognized some good had been gained with the knowledge I now had; regardless, I could not help but wonder if it would have been possible to obtain this knowledge and gain without such a travesty of justice taking place. Several peers and members of audiences would come up to me and tell me my story inspired them to remain positive about problems they were experiencing. There were moments, too, when looking at small children, tears would unexpectedly flow, and I would think about their learning someday how evil some people could be. I wanted to protect them from learning the things I now knew had pervaded our country: the debasing of innocence caused by envy, moral chaos, violence, and drugs as well as the corruptions within our political and legal systems. I wanted them to retain (and me to be able to go back to) the beliefs people would treat others as they wished to be treated and others could be trusted. I also wanted, of course, for them to never experience the pain at others' hands as I had. How foolish? No, how sad!

The hardest part of the aftermath was maintaining a positive attitude as consequences continued to come in the years following Selma's false allegations. I was determined not to let the Medifraud unit win twice; that is, if I gave in to the depression or completely gave up my private practice, I would have thought myself defeated. Depression would have hurt my family even more than they had been hurt. The money I lost was not as important to me as my faith and my family. I did not want to fall into the victimization role, ending up bitter and resentful. I perceived the actions of Darrell, Jazelle, Lee, Marvin, and Selma the results of their falling into that role, and I did not want my behavior to cause the kind of devastation their actions had.

The corporation was dissolved, and the offices for which I held mortgages were put up for sale or rent. I believed, without the additional costs of maintaining a corporation, I might be able to salvage my private practice and avoid bankruptcy. After the corporation dissolved, I resolved to pay off all my debts no matter how long it took. My background of fairness was such, I was determined no one else would suffer the legitimate loss of funds through a personal bankruptcy proceeding or one for the corporation. I considered it to be unfair for this to happen to others, as a result of what had happened to me, if I could possibly prevent it. I hoped my husband and I would not have to lose our home, but for a while, it looked as if the legal costs might force the sale of our modest home, should the additional costs of private practice continue to mount. Saving our home had been a significant factor in the decision to plea bargain. Further, I was learning how futile my beliefs were when it came to legal contracts being protectors of my rights. They might be judged legal at the end of a suit, but defending a suit still cost money. Out-of-court settlements often ended with both sides paying their legal fees; thus, neither attorney incurred much risk when some wanted to sue another party. This was true, especially for nuisance, ludicrous, or frivolous suits.

Nonetheless, without even a receptionist to help, I now had unbelievable stress from telephone calls made and received to conclude the business of the corporation while seeing a few patients. Although my practice was now less than part time, there were bills to be paid—utilities, mortgages, loans, telephone expenses, real estate taxes, liability insurance, and so on. Thus, I began tutoring for ten dollars an hour and teaching part-time classes to pay the bills. It was even harder to maintain my sanity when I would receive letters from insurance companies indicating they had paid for services in error because the patient had had a pre-existing condition. I would be required to refund the payment or be sued for it. Many times, this would occur a year after the patient left therapy. Efforts to have the patient reimburse me then were difficult, sometimes futile, and always unfair to the patient. Therefore, I usually wrote off the bill.

In addition, several business contracts had misleading clauses that claimed I was responsible for services beyond the date of cancellation or the dissolving of a business. One example was the offices' alarm system monitoring. A couple of months after the anniversary date of the contract, the bill for payment arrived. The corporation had a five-year contract. There was a clause that said it was automatically renewed at the end of the contract for two years. So, before the date I was to pay for the following years' service, I cancelled the service. After all, the one unit was completely empty and, when the unit was installed, it was incorrectly installed to monitor both units together and was disengaged in the empty unit. Selling or renting only that unit would make the alarm system impractical, and I did not have the funds at that time to have it reinstalled. Obviously, the company would not acknowledge their error when it was installed. To my surprise, I received a bill for the two-year period for which it was to be automatically renewed even though there was to be no service given. This was eventually cleared up. I learned from a bankruptcy attorney many persons under the type of stress I was experiencing would have paid it without realizing it. Two years later, when the statute of limitations had passed, one might get an apology. It was numerous problems such as these that added to the incredible stress. I now was working over eighty hours a week again in an effort to try to stay on top of the bills and to avoid bankruptcy.

It seemed a never-ending battle. When I began to see some progress, however, it was worth the struggle. I did not lose my home, and while the corporation was qualified to file bankruptcy, it did not. I chipped away at the debts a little at a time by living frugally. I worked with some of my creditors to avoid getting a poor credit rating. The mortgage on the one unit was eventually paid off; this helped make the overhead expenses more manageable and bankruptcy no longer a threat. While I was working on getting my financial situation under control, I studied amateur radio and passed my license exam. That way Connie and I could communicate with each other several times during the day. He would come to my office, and we would have lunch whenever we could. We were determined to spend as much time as we could together in spite of the work I was required to do to survive the losses the investigation had brought about. He supported my decision to avoid bankruptcy. Most of all, he frequently let me know how proud he was of my efforts to regain my success as a private practitioner and reminded me how few could have overcome the problems I had overcome. His support was priceless to me.

The poor financial situation and decreased cash flow, which had continued for so long, had added considerable tension and strain to my life, and that stress finally caught up with me. I had had several medical problems during the years following the betrayal. Three years after the nightmare began, I was diagnosed with cancer, requiring major surgery, chemotherapy, and additional medical bills. I believe my husband's death, if not caused by this travesty, was accelerated by it. Continuing to practice after his death was the hardest thing I had ever done in my life. No one can imagine the difficulty I was having as I attempted to remain optimistic and positive when sinking into despair and hopelessness would have been so much easier. Again, I credit my deep faith for pulling me through.

Through this experience with the Medifraud unit and the legal system, I gained an in-depth understanding of post-traumatic stress disorder (PTSD) and the aftermath of abuse, trauma, or injustice at the hands of another person. Coupled with training, my personal knowledge gave me the skills to work with PTSD persons and victims of crime. Satisfied patients told referral sources about me. The result was an increase in patient load and, thus, in income. Nonetheless, the changes in third-party benefits due to the health care crisis, the recession, and rising costs of maintaining a private practice did not return me to the same success I knew before I met Darrell. However, I was beginning to meet my bills and, with a few hundred dollars left over, make a modest living. I recall being almost ecstatic when I bought my first new dress in eight years.

At this time, I live in the home the plea bargain saved. I am grateful it was ours when Connie died. Nonetheless, without my precious husband to share it with me, the victory is both hollow and bittersweet. Furthermore, it took a long time to overcome all of the pain and fear of a dreadful, nightmarish experience. There are times when I remember it, and the hurt is ever fresh. However, the hurt does not control me; the knowledge gained keeps me cautious. I can see much good that has come of it. I believe I am a much stronger person because of living through it. Thus, although I had forgiven those who caused my hell, I did not regain enough trust in the legal and governmental systems to resume my previous private practice clinic. The decision to remain a sole practitioner was difficult to maintain. However, I had the assistance of the receptionist and office manager, and, by retaining contracts with an accountant and a medical billing company, I was helped considerably to make a modest living. So, when I thought working alone impeded my effectiveness, I enjoyed meeting with colleagues; I would come away restored, refreshed, and motivated to continue my efforts. Besides, I truly wanted to continue my vocation of seeing the patients who came to me and assisting them to overcome some of life's struggles. After selling the office and closing my practice, I worked for a company that provided services to nursing homes the last five years of my career. This was a blessing for me because I did not have to deal with scheduling patients and billing insurance companies. I was able to retire at age seventy. After retiring, I volunteered at a hospital for ten years. This was most gratifying for me as I continued to retain friendships with so many of those I had worked with over my career.

CHAPTER TEN

EDUCATING FELLOW MENTAL HEALTH PROFESSIONALS AND THE PUBLIC ABOUT THE PROBLEM

———————❋———————

I remained appalled by the amount of damage vindictive ex-employees could cause some, appalled by a legal system that promoted it, and even more appalled at the treatment I received from persons in my own profession and other professionals. Thus, when I began hearing and reading about similar suits taking place around the United States, my anger became energized. I communicated with a reporter on the *Psychiatric Times* and officers of the Practice Directorate Office of the APA. I was instrumental in bringing about the uniting of national professional organizations, primarily the APA and American Psychiatric Association (APsyA) to look into the matter. (This was a rare happening itself.) After a meeting in Washington, DC, with members of both groups, attorneys who had represented a couple of targeted practitioners and several of us who had been victims of abuse, a joint letter was sent by these mental health organizations to Richard P. Kusserow, then the inspector general of the Department of Health and Human Services. (See Appendix A.) Inspector General Kusserow also was responsible for both the funding and the monitoring of the Medicaid

Fraud Control Units throughout the United States. Articles began to appear in major psychiatric and psychological publications apprising readers of possible abuses they faced from Medifraud offices. More importantly, the State quota requirement for prosecutions of health professionals was removed.

A trip to Washington, DC, had resulted in much needed support as well as initiating strategies for investigating the travesty of justice taking place in at least ten of the thirty-nine states where Medicaid/Medicare fraud units were established, federally funded, and given conviction quotas. Huge fines given to those convicted were major sources of their funding, thereby justifying the continued existence of fraud units. I agreed to testify before a Senate Committee, if necessary. After a lengthy delay in responding to the letter sent to him, Inspector General Kusserow said the problem should be addressed at the state level because it was not a national problem. In a follow-up correspondence regarding the evasiveness of his answer, he replied that his office did not employ people to "supervise or provide oversight" to Medifraud units of those thirty-nine states. (See Appendix A.) The *Monitor* (published through APA) wrote an article in January 1990 to apprise members of their decision to look into the matter and to be available for support until something official could be done. The *Psychiatric Times* wrote an article in February 1990 summarizing many of the efforts made to that date. Names of persons they could contact in APA and APsyA were given for providers who might be experiencing similar problems or be concerned about what was happening to their professional peers. Providers were encouraged to contact them if they had any questions as well as to obtain information to protect them from being targeted. I felt a mixture of joy and sadness; I thought my efforts would prevent what had happened to me from happening to other mental health professions, but it was too late to be of help to me.

Themes of the letter sent to Inspector General Kusserow were:

1. Apparent constitutional due process violations and harassment by state investigators;

2. Disregard for therapist-patient confidentiality by state investigators;
3. Criminal fraud charges based on minor technical violations of the Medicaid procedures, such as coding errors by providers, or based on ambiguities of the Medicaid laws and regulations;
4. A resulting type of "double jeopardy" whereby providers are first prosecuted under criminal penalties and then followed by a similar process for civil penalties for the same charges. (*Psychiatric Times*, February 1990.)

Even these words, devoid of emotions, cannot describe the terrible feelings of helplessness those of us felt who had experienced the abusive prosecutions. With all of the "support" we were receiving, no funds were being used to challenge them or to reimburse us for the tremendous losses we had endured. We also were being told that, realistically, little could be done with a system that had become so corrupt. As Ronald Schwartz, JD, reportedly apprised the attendants of the 1990 APsyA annual meeting:

> Motivation to find physicians guilty of Medicaid fraud involves more than the legitimate goal of uncovering fraud in the Medicaid system.... With Medicaid expected to consume 25 percent of state budgets within five years, the system is under pressure to keep costs to a minimum.... To put money back into the Medicaid system, U.S. Inspector General Richard Kusserow had, until recently, assigned investigators an annual conviction target number.... Failure to reach the quota means no promotion. (*Psychiatric Times*, July 1990.)

Those attending the meeting left knowing legislative solutions to the abusive investigative practices were going to be as difficult to obtain as would be the reformations of the system that brought them about. Private practitioners would continue to be targeted because it cost much more to investigate large clinics and hospitals. Not only would clinics and hospitals be able to afford better defenses, but the fraud units would not want to risk spending a lot of money and time and end up unable to prove intent to commit fraud; it was easier to convince a jury that one person had motive for fraud but not several persons within a hospital staff. We were told at a later date our best approach was to concentrate on finding ways to unite our efforts. For example, when all practitioners in one state were willing to treat Medicaid patients and temporarily not bill for their charges, it got the news media's attention to the underlying reasons for their actions. They then were able to demonstrate how the investigations had made a mockery out of the system and illustrated how such criminal investigations were not cost effective for the overall program; they were designed to destroy the very professionals whose work primarily was to help the taxpayers and not bilk the system. This effort was counteracted by the Federal Department of Health and Human Services coming out with a new regulation; not billing for services was considered a way of avoiding investigation and thereby illegal. As is often true, there were a few professionals who did try to bilk the system and some who were committing fraud; the actions of a few had jeopardized the innocence of many. Battle-wearied practitioners were so disillusioned by the lack of peer support, they were unwilling to unite their efforts anymore. Instead, many concentrated on finding other types of work.

During the meeting in Washington, the senators emphasized the importance of educating other psychiatrists and psychologists that they needed to supervise the billing of their services more closely. Mental health professionals had been chosen to be targeted for the abusive prosecutions, according to the former inspector general of the Department of Health and Human Services, because the laws governing the reimbursement of mental health services were so vague. Moreover, it was more difficult for doctors to substantiate the rationale for charges. This made it easy for huge fines to be levied against them for minute infractions of complicated procedures. It was unlikely providers would decide to give the services free of charge (even temporarily to make their point) and risk huge fines and the loss of their livelihood. Not only that, but few could afford to do this for as many people who required Medicaid/

Medicare services and remain in private practice. Besides, the little understood provision in the mental health laws that made them eligible for prosecution for providing free services was a deterrent. According to Medicaid/Medicare rules, this was an effort to avoid investigation. Free clinics and volunteer charitable organized foundations were exempt. Thus, even if there were practitioners who were willing to provide services free to them, persons on government assistance eventually could be forced to go to a governmentally funded mental health clinic. At such clinics, they might receive inferior or inadequate care. This would be due to the numbers seeking assistance and the minimal pay scale, which would not attract the more qualified personnel. Thus, most mental health professionals would not want to risk the consequences of this type of action.

Believing articles in the professional papers could not answer specific questions, and to alert mental health providers of the vastness of the problem, the APA and APsyA representatives at the meetings encouraged us to give workshops and lectures describing potential dangers private practitioners faced. The national organizations promised to sponsor the workshops and to provide the necessary materials. In exchange, some of the monies obtained would be used in a senate presentation of the problem. I provided such a workshop in my area as did others. As we predicted, in order to protect ourselves from further prosecutor retaliations, we could not give sufficient information in the invitations, so these workshops were poorly attended. We were, after all, the outcasts with our professional colleagues. Other workshops were organized, however, and presented at the annual meetings of both organizations and the annual meeting of the American Medical Association (AMA); these were better attended.

Those of us who had been victims of Medifraud investigations were not surprised by the complacency of fellow professionals and lack of interest to attend local workshops. Many of us admitted that, prior to our victimizations, we would have responded in much the same way. We already had experienced being ostracized by colleagues, so the lack of interest of colleagues to learn what had and could continue to occur was not as surprising to us as it was to the national officers of the two organizations. One colleague whom I once considered a friend told me the workshop invitation sounded too aggressive and I should give it free of charge anyway. I silently laughed at the ridiculousness of his statements when I hung up the telephone. Where did he think the funds to provide workshops would come from? This was a man who did little free and yet was suggesting I should do so. When I talked with the Washington APA office, similar responses from others were reported. Thus, when the national conferences were held, seminars for providers to learn how to protect themselves from being investigated were included. At least those attending the annual conferences could be alerted to the state of affairs. Even so, they were not as well attended as anticipated. Some participants voiced their belief they doubted it could happen to them as they were more careful about their offices' procedures since they had been reading about the investigations. Unless and until suits were filed for ending the abuse-of-power tactics, those of us who had been victimized were considered to be insignificant practitioners. We could not reveal all the information we had, except when protected by confidentiality, because of further possible repercussions against us. We were apprised the procedures could take years. Meanwhile, most victims lost their reputations, their livelihoods, and any retirement savings they had. In addition, some committed suicide and several lost families, their homes, and many cherished possessions.

A television documentary hosted by Barbara Walters, *Who Watches the Watchdogs*, was scheduled by one national network to begin alerting the public of the scam. Even though some recipients, doctors, and hospitals did bilk Medicaid/Medicare funds, it was important the public be told most did not and some investigations were unwarranted. Administration costs of the Medicaid/Medicare programs had skyrocketed and were bilking the system far more than the recipients and providers. Salaries for unneeded positions as well as huge salaries for the upper management positions were a significant drain on available monies. One way to avoid the public recognizing how persons in administrative positions were skimming the tax dollars for their own personal gains was to focus on doctors. The public already thought they were rich and were easily duped into believing they were crooked as well. The Medifraud offices also were spending much money on promoting articles for health journals and popular magazines designed to obtain public outcry against the unscrupulous doctors, thereby further misleading the public and ensuring any doctor brought to trial would be convicted. Nonetheless, by continuing to tell the public the truth, we hoped the truth would eventually be heard.

Suggestions for improving the program administration and the costs of the Medicaid/Medicare programs were made. Since then, the four major issues mentioned in the letter to Inspector General Kusserow have been addressed but not entirely eliminated. The pyramid model of most bureaucracies, especially government bureaucracies, remained a major waste of time, procedures, and personnel costs. Therefore, one answer is to place the programs in the jurisdiction of the states. Even so, it must be revamped and streamlined to avoid waste and to ensure the majority of monies goes to recipients and those who provide the needed services.

CHAPTER ELEVEN

HINDSIGHT ANATOMY

———— ✳ ————

*A*s I looked back over the drama of those dreadful years, I had to recognize the behaviors in myself that had contributed to my initial victimization by making me vulnerable to be targeted for an investigation by the Medifraud units. I had to take responsibility for the decisions and actions that I made that permitted others to take advantage of the situation. When I hired Darrell as well as other employees, I had been too absorbed in my desire to help others that I did not pay attention or acknowledge warnings I should have heeded. When Darrell talked about the growth of the clinic, he appealed to elements of egotistic pride within me, and I envisioned my success. When I was physically and emotionally drained from the investigation and an associate offered to help out by supervising Darrell, I chose to ignore the opportunistic tendencies in him, which had prevented me from completely trusting him in the past. As such, that he would look for an opportunity to take over the branch office should not have surprised me. That my attorney, the judge, or my former employees would be more concerned with their own interests and reputations rather than mine was natural. Indeed, ignoring the Golden Rule was a sign of the times. Just as the '80s were said to be a time of selfish affluence, the '90s were the age of greed and envy. (Jane Ciabattari, "Will the '90s be the Age of Envy," *Psychology Today*, pp. 46-50.) Certainly, those who had misrepresented me were responding in normal ways for the times, and, their personalities should have alerted me of this. Furthermore, I disregarded some of the changes being brought about by increased health insurance costs, organization of health plans, dissatisfactions among mental health providers, and effects of inflation on employee attitudes.

I further had to acknowledge that my being naïve about the legal system and processes of being sued or having charges brought against a person did not permit me to make reasonable and informed decisions at each step of the way. I should not have blindly trusted the attorney I had used for the years I had incorporated the clinic to represent me in such a complicated case. I did so because he said he had worked with another Medicaid case and I knew him to be a trustworthy person. I learned later that he and the judge were friends and, when the case clearly became a witch hunt, the judge had encouraged my attorney to get it settled out of court as quickly as he could. Neither of them had wanted to deal with it any longer than necessary. Thus, it would have been more prudent to have taken the time and spent the money to find an attorney with more experience dealing with the bureaucracies of government and with the Medicaid/Medicare system in particular.

Not finding a different attorney had three major ramifications: (1) Because of my decreased emotional state of mind, I depended too much on the suggestions of my attorney, which were based on the usual and logical consequences of legal maneuvers and a lack of knowledge of how competitive mental health professionals were. This, in turn, provided a fertile ground for the relentless Medicops to work within. Unable to think clearly, I remained in disbelief and shock about what really was happening. (2) Instead of asking for a continuance while I looked for a new attorney, I continued to spend monies to defend my innocence while not using any legal recourse to delay a trial or to reverse the conviction on my record. (3) I relinquished my right to go to trial and to have three judges presiding over it. Instead, because I did not know there was an alternative, I believed my attorney when he said it was doubtful I could get a fair trial since I would not have a jury of real peers. It seemed my future was sacrificed for the reputations of my attorney and the judge before whom I appeared. Neither wanted to fight a government agency; such an action could portray them as radical, thereby blemishing their political aspirations.

Two years after making the fateful decision of accepting the Medifraud office's plea bargain offer, I realized that convicted violent killers had more rights than I did to appeal their convictions. The only legal method by which I could reverse the decision (according to my lawyer) was to fire him, sue him, and begin the process all over again. In other words, by stating that my lawyer did not properly or sufficiently advise me, another attorney could sue for legal costs and damages. If I won a favorable decision through a trial, then the decision would be reversed and my legal costs paid. (I was not so naïve by this time to believe it would be easy to find another attorney who would be willing to discredit a colleague. In spite of my experiences with other psychologists, I was certain attorneys were much more supportive of each other than were psychologists.) Later, another suit against the Medifraud unit for abusive investigation could bring about my receiving a settlement. If I lost and received an unfavorable decision, not only would I have to pay for all the additional legal expenses, which could be triple or more what I had already paid, but I could also be in a more precarious and adverse position legally and professionally than before. The risks were many times over the previous ones. Usually being conservative by nature, I continued following what I thought was the surer route.

Initially, my husband and I had labored under the delusion that the Medifraud investigation would be conducted fairly and reasonably. He traveled to Columbus with the attorney for a meeting with the state prosecutor; they had reams of documents substantiating the coding problems, administrative difficulties of the Medicaid/Medicare program, and proof there was no intent to commit fraud on my part. The state prosecutor seemed most upset by a letter written by the governor apologizing for the problems providers were having billing for services and stating efforts were being made to simplify the forms and to cut down on the required paperwork. The prosecutor voiced the recognition that it would be most difficult to prove fraud; yet a few months after the meeting, he was offering the plea bargain to save taxpayer monies. We realized many months later, he had been covering up his expensive efforts to investigate the ridiculous allegations of a vindictive fired employee. When I voiced my concern about the stress of all Connie was doing to aid the attorney, my husband told me he could not have handled what was happening to me unless he did everything he could to help. He said standing by helpless was much worse than the stress of doing whatever he could to aid in bringing a close to the nightmare we were experiencing. Truly, the considerable time and efforts made by my husband were significant contributors to his heart condition, but he said it would have been a small price to pay had the results of his work been examined in the court. Nonetheless, his work was invaluable when we went to Washington to substantiate the claims of abusive investigative procedures.

A case, sadder than my own, was reviewed the following year. Again, I had naively believed the facts in this case were flagrantly obvious and would demonstrate the maliciousness of Medifraud investigations. The psychologist was a former Psychology Board president who had worked very hard to promote the interests of all psychologists. He had been instrumental in bringing about the ability of psychological supervisees serving their final internships before going into private practice to treat welfare patients. Just as he was preparing to retire, one of his former supervisees was being investigated for improper treatment of welfare patients. To avoid major penalties and to lessen his convictions, he alleged he had not been properly supervised when he worked under that psychologist. The allegations and uncovered evidence were all circumstantial and probably would not have stood up in court. The former Board president was then investigated, and the procedures closely followed those used in my case. Again, the motivations of the complaining person were not considered. He, too, was offered the plea bargain to save taxpayer monies and forced to pay a huge fine. When I called him to offer understanding and support, he was in tears, and expressed his appreciation for my call. I met with him and apprised him of what might occur because he blindly believed his colleagues would stand by him. He, too, told me their failure to do so was the most devastating experience of his career. Needless to say, he lost his livelihood and retirement funds and could not afford a reasonable defense. He was ordered as a part of his punishment to write open letters of apology in the paper and in a profession magazine! For him, that was the final straw that sent him into a deep depression, and he committed suicide. What ignominy the Medifraud prosecutor put upon him! Five years later, I was to learn, indirectly, another professional attributed his public apology to me in his effort to place doubt in a colleague's mind about me.

Several incorrect stories circulated. Some, who did not have the courage, respect, or decency to speak to me about what had really happened but wanted to appear knowledgeable about what had taken place, gave their own version of the investigation. Most of this was gossip and incorrect. Once, when I called my attorney about a slanderous story, he called the person who had given serious incorrect information and told him that, continuing to speak about a situation where they were so misinformed could result in a slander suit. I knew; however, I could not sue everyone who was gossiping about me, nor would I want to do so. Moreover, it would be difficult to disprove such statements; I hoped most people would categorize them as hearsay.

At one point, I consulted an attorney to examine my case with regard to challenging whether or not my constitutional rights had been violated or ignored by the Medifraud unit, especially my rights to be given due process and to avoid double jeopardy. Although I had a reasonable chance to win the case, primarily because of all the evidence substantiating my innocence obtained by my husband and the results of the investigations of similar cases, I did not have the funds to present my case. My request of APA to sponsor a class action suit ended with a rejection from them to help. They did not believe enough psychologists and members of APA would benefit in proportion to the hundreds of thousands of dollars required for such a suit to take place. This determination was made in spite of the fact that each year numerous psychologists had lost their licenses to practice psychology and, hence, their membership in APA. APA further determined a better use of the money needed to sponsor a class action suit would be to increase educational efforts, alerting psychologists to the dangers along with suggestions of how to avoid a similar investigation. Once again, I was forced to face the unfair fact that justice belongs only to those who can afford it; hardly a part of the American legacy I had been taught to believe was for all.

Telephone calls to the American Civil Liberties Union were not fruitful. Not only were their cases backlogged so that they would be unable to take the case for several months or years, but the existing abuses of billing for excessive treatment and sometimes unneeded procedures by physicians and surgeons made them skeptical they could win the case. Moreover, they wanted landmark cases, which would protect many who could not afford legal assistance and which would settle controversial issues. Doctors accused of fraud may not have fallen into either category. For me, I had hit another barrier I could not overcome.

As time went on, I realized the attorney I approached to examine my case for violation of my constitutional rights was chairman of the local mental health board, which meant she would be aligned with the Medifraud unit. When her name and a couple of other attorneys specializing in constitutional law had been given to me by another attorney, he suggested my case had such merit as to be a case that an attorney likely would take on consignment because of the potential publicity helpful to an attorney's career. He was not a specialist in constitutional law as they were or he would have taken the case himself. He said he was that certain the case would be won in my favor. When I read the name of the attorney I had approached as being aligned with the very unit which had persecuted me, I wondered where her ethics were. Should she not have told me my case reflected a conflict of interest? Had she inflated the number of hours and, hence the cost, to represent me before the national administrative and judicial committees such that the APA would more likely refuse to sponsor the case? Had she informed the Medifraud unit that they need not worry about being sued because I could not afford to challenge their office's tactics? Had she given them information that alerted them how to change those tactics to avoid other suits? As I pondered those questions and other similar ones, chills ran through my body. As I shared my thoughts with family and friends, they and I felt a revolting disgust at our legal system. I lost all trust in obtaining fairness in a system promoting a sham of justice. Interest in the demise of the legal system was a frequent subject of conversation at several professional staff meetings that I attended. The public was given several opportunities to realize how out of control the legal system had become through television dramatizations of the cases of people who had been subjects of a travesty as documentaries such as the one on ABC's *Day One* on June 14, 1993. Many people felt a sense of hopelessness. How could there be any chance for reform of the legal system when the majority of politicians and those in a position to do something about it were lawyers themselves?

Nonetheless, throughout those past few incredibly painful years, I learned much about myself and what was most important to me in life. Although I struggled to have some of the things I had worked so hard to have in my retirement years, was unable to retire before I was seventy, and was unable to spend the time with my husband as we had planned to enjoy together, the future had something to offer. There were days when that future was harder to accept; those were the days when the loss of my husband made all other problems pale. Regardless, I had my children and grandchildren to enjoy. I had regained a lucrative practice and overcome serious physical, professional, and financial obstacles. Most of all, the treasure of the support, love, and loyalty of those among my family, friends, and patients who stood by me during the darkest of times could never be replaced by all the money in the world. While I would not have willingly chosen what happened to me or hired those who betrayed me had I been able to see into the future, I did not hate them or blame them. I daily prayed for them and wished no harm to come to them. They must live with themselves and be accountable for their actions. Only a higher being can see into their hearts and judge their deeds. I repeated frequently The Prayer to the Holy Spirit (See Appendix B), to obtain the divine gift to forgive and forget all that others do to one, as I sought emotional healing. As far as I was concerned, I was at peace with the knowledge justice has always been in God's hands, and I did all I could to right the wrongs done to me.

CHAPTER TWELVE

WILL RIGHT PREVAIL?

─────────── ✳ ───────────

*A*s time went on, more information sifted in about the treatment other psychologists and psychiatrists had received from Medicaid Fraud Units. In addition to suits filed by psychologists and psychiatrists in Hawaii, New York, and New Jersey (to name a few states so involved), a class action suit was filed by non-Medicaid patients of a psychiatrist in Utah for invasion of their privacy and for interfering with their treatment as a result of an investigation of their psychiatrist. The patients deemed tactics used in the investigation were abuses of power and disregarded their civil rights as well as the psychiatrist's civil rights. Two Massachusetts psychiatrists publicly accused the Medicaid Unit chief of misconduct. Another psychiatrist in New Jersey brought charges after he was found not guilty in trial of the fraud for which he had been indicted. The Medical Society of the State of New York (MSSNY) began one of the first defending actions against the New York Medifraud unit for using inappropriate tactics, rationales, and procedures while investigating a psychiatrist in that state. The list goes on. Some of these cases, which after years were brought to closure, supported the allegations of wrongful prosecution. These usually dealt with mental health practitioners who did not give into plea bargaining tactics and were subsequently cleared of charges. As a result of the pressure put on APsyA by members who had been victimized by the Medifraud units and who had subsequently been convicted, the APsyA began assisting the psychiatrists in their efforts to clear their names and regain some of the damages. Most, however, did not obtain that support; they had chosen to plea-bargain because they could not afford the cost of going on to trial. Others were attempting to obtain sufficient monies to appeal questionable convictions of fraud while maintaining an innocence of wrongful intent. Similar actions by the APA were not forthcoming for psychologists who had been caught up in the travesty of justice committed by Medicaid fraud units.

Nonetheless, the undermining of public trust in mental health practitioners as well as the mistrust of government officials appointed to protect public concerns were two major problems. The abuse-of-power tactics of Medifraud units largely contributed to these problems. Just as the few who bilked the Medicaid/Medicare system must take some responsibility for the zeal with which the fraud unit officials pursued their objectives, so too must any person in public office (professional or governmental) recognize abusing their power will undermine the trust level of most citizens. It is unfortunate that human beings can be influenced by evil just as by good. Helping people differentiate between good and evil motives has been a struggle for leaders since the civilized world began and will continue to be so. Due to this important factor, I was convinced that any government committee commissioned, to look into the probability of abusive prosecution and to outline corrective procedures, needed to keep this in mind.

The senators and the representatives of the national psychological and psychiatric organizations present at the Washington meeting emphasized that the overzealousness of the fraud squads could not be repeated any more. The senators cautioned that, as we began the fight to try to right the wrong done to mental health practitioners in the malicious prosecution cases across the country, we should not become vindictive in return. We were encouraged to be factual as much as possible and as nonjudgmental as we could be without weakening our positions or diluting the importance of reversing the wrongful consequences of many inappropriate indictments. This book has attempted to reflect that intent. Professionals who had been victimized were encouraged by national mental health organizations to attend several support conferences. Upon returning to home locales, some organized public lectures for the purposes of educating public and professional communities. It was the consensus of the whole group present at the meeting that we hoped press releases could be reviewed by a senate committee and the officers of the professional organizations so that what was published would be mutually agreeable. It was suggested by a senator, and agreed upon by the group, that we invite persons, who had been used by the fraud units to convict doctors, to attend private meetings where confrontations and communication could take place safely. The names of the persons were to be kept confidential if they preferred this. Any information leaving the meetings would be screened to avoid misinterpretation and continued undermining of the Medicaid/Medicare system both for the providers and the recipients. As far as I knew, those who have been victimized have not followed through with these suggestions. I did not know their reasons. I only knew mine. Without the support of colleagues and financial backing of the APA, such meetings would have been fruitless. Besides, I still feared any backlash to my efforts.

Two years after the meetings in Washington and the hurting cries of the wounded were heard, investigations of doctors committing fraud were fewer. No more suits were being considered to examine whether there had been constitutional due process violations, harassment by investigators, double jeopardy violations, or cruel and unjust punishment rendered. The media seldom reported such abuse. It was as if it no longer was taking place. The focus, though crucially important, was on spiraling health care costs, the inability of many to obtain health insurance, expanding Medicaid/Medicare benefits, and increasing the number of recipients who would be eligible. Many were concerned about where the additional funds would be obtained to pay for these. Occasionally one might read about how frustrated a welfare recipient would become if they tried to return monies they had erroneously received. They would learn the system was so inefficient and mismanaged that checks would continue coming long after they had notified case managers of the situation; some would give up and then be charged with fraud for accepting monies they were not entitled to receive.

There were other cases wherein persons needing assistance and being qualified became homeless and destitute while the bureaucratic wheels turned slowly. The public became disgusted with banking industry scandals, the Congressional bounced-check fiasco mudslinging during political campaigns and government officials in general; little trust and respect remained of those in positions of authority. As the talk of national health care accelerated, certain momentous questions needed consideration. Would the same administrative personnel be in charge? Would the internal corruption not only continue but expand? Would health care of the poor be jeopardized more while the heads of insurance and pharmaceutical companies received enormous salaries and benefits? Would middle class citizens receive adequate and quality care or would only the upper class and rich be able to afford such care? How could health care costs be prevented from spiraling when huge unlimited settlements for malpractice suits continued to be awarded?

The representatives of the national professional organizations hoped the methods used to heal the wounds caused by the unfortunate chain of events brought about by the Medifraud units' abuses of power would portray the American justice system at its best. It had been hoped, too, that the nonjudgmental tactics used would demonstrate sensationalism in news reporting did not serve citizens well. Instead of this, the Medifraud units appeared to almost stop their unfair tactics. This seemed good, and I and my colleagues wanted to be pleased, but those of us most intimately involved wondered who the next targets would be. Moreover, we would have been more gratified if the system had finally worked and right had prevailed for each of us. Regardless of what was to come and whether or not some compensation would be forthcoming for the price each of us paid, at least we knew, for a time anyway, fewer would be as mistreated as we were. What continued to frighten us was the knowledge fraudulent suits would begin again when the public had forgotten the past and the administration costs noticeably depleted funds once more.

On May 10, 1992, *Sixty Minutes* presented a program about the number of disillusioned physicians who were leaving the health care fields and discouraging others from going into it. The physicians said they were no longer willing to spend twelve to twenty years with sparse income and difficult study to prepare for a profession that no longer was fulfilling their desires to help people. The return now was vast amounts of paperwork, Medifraud investigations, and less compensation than most other professional fields. One of my physician friends commented when we talked about the program:

> Sometimes I get angry, knowing that no matter how much I pay my staff, it is never enough. Like those who took everything away from you, there are those who want all I have without working for it or sacrificing to get it. Do they have any idea of the commitment I had to make to ensure they have a job which pays them well? There are days I would like to pack it all in and leave medicine and I have to remind myself of the reasons I chose to become a physician in the first place.

I, too, wondered how many knew how little I earned in comparison to the commitment I had to make and the sacrifices I had made to be able to do what I did well. I had continued to practice my skills even after the terrible nightmare had happened because I knew I was helping others to cope with difficult times in their lives. I truly loved my patients and wanted things to be better for them. So, I smiled at my colleague's words and related the memory I had of a time when I had taken my employees out to lunch. It was an example of the subtle way in which my self-esteem had been slowly fractured even before the betrayal took place. Of the nine of us who had gone out to lunch that day, I was the only one with a doctorate. Yet the waitress called Darrell "doctor" and appeared to assume I worked for him. Darrell said it was not important and I would look foolish if I corrected the misperception. The waitress seemed only slightly embarrassed when I paid the bill with a credit card and signed my name with the doctorate title. Even so, as I had watched the program and again as we discussed it, I felt the pain of knowing jealousy was a likely motivator for what had happened to me. I then told my colleague that, in spite of all their efforts, no one had nor could anyone take away the most important elements in my life: faith, family, and friends.

This book, which you have been gracious and patient enough to read, was written so that you could understand my experience and recognize its pain and subsequent healing. I was one of many who suffered because of the consequences of others' choices in a fractured world. The pain was intense and more severe than any other pain I previously had experienced. Some symptoms of PSTD remain with me, such as hypervigilance and nightmares as well as a timidity to speak up in self-defense and uncomfortable feelings when confronted by others (especially men) in a demeaning or authoritative tone of voice. Even today, when I recall the events I have written about, I find it hard to believe it really happened to me. The treatment I eventually received from some was just as warm and pleasurable. The light at the end of tunnel grows brighter as time goes on, and the many who walked with me have hopefully gained insight into how well things can turn out when belief in others, forgiveness, and optimism replace greed, false pride, and vindictive righteousness. I still think this dream is possible, but not probable, in this world.

REFERENCES

———————✳———————

Ciabattari, J. (1989, December). "Are the 1980's the age of envy?"

Psychology Today, pp, 46-50.

Fishman, H. (1990, February). "Associations Unite to Look into Alleged Medicaid Fraud Investigation Abuses." *The Psychiatric Times,* Santa Ana, CA: A CME Publication, Inc., Publication, p, 56.

Schwartz, R., J.D. (1990, July). *The Psychiatric Times,* Santa Ana, CA: A CME Publication, Inc., Publication, p. 25.

Subby, R. (1984). <u>Codependency, An Emerging Issue</u>. Hollywood, FL: Health Communications, p. 25.

BIBLIOGRAPHY

———————✳———————

AARP Bulletin. (Monthly Newspaper). Various articles from 1990 through 1993. Washington, DC: American Association of Retired Persons.

Blade. Various articles from 1990 through 1998. Toledo, Ohio.

Brown, C.A. (1988, February 4). "Don't give in to a Medifraud goon squad." *Medical Economics*, pp. 232-247.

Castro, J. (1991, November 25). "Condition: Critical." *Time*, pp. 34-42.

Christian Prayer: The Liturgy of the Hours. (1985, 1976). NY: Catholic Book Publishing Co.

Ciabattari, J. (1989, December). "Are the 1980's the age of envy?" *Psychology Today*, pp, 46-50.

Independent Practitioner, The. (Monthly Bulletin). Phoenix, AZ: American Psychological Association, Division of Independent Practice.

Lerner, H. (1985). *The Dance of Anger*. NY: Harper & Row.

Medicaid/Medicare Providers Handbook. (1988). Columbus, OH: Nationwide Mutual Insurance Company, Medicare Operations.

Medicare Newsletters. (1986 through 1989). Columbus, OH: Nationwide Mutual Insurance Company, Medicare Operations.

Monitor. (Monthly Newspaper). Various articles from 1989 through 1992. Washington, DC: American Psychological Association Publication.

O'Connell, Rev. J.D. (ed.). (1952). *The Holy Bible*. Chicago, IL: The Catholic Press, Inc.

Peck, N.S. (1983), *People of the Lie*. NY: Simon & Schuster, Inc.

Psychiatric Times, The. (Monthly Newspaper). Various articles from 1988 through 1991. Santa Ana, CA: A CME, Inc., Publication.

Quinn, J.B. (1992, February 24). "When Health Plans Fail." *Newsweek*, p. 45.

Starks, S. (1988, July 4). "To the Medicops, there are no honest mistakes." *Medical Economics*, pp. 52-57.

Subby, R. (1984). *Codependency, An Emerging Issue*. Hollywood, FL: Health Communications.

Tavris, C. (1992, October). "The New Witch-Hunts." *Redbook*, p. 49.

"Who Pays for Health Care?" *Block News Alliance Special Series*. (1991, December 22-27). Toledo, OH: Blade.

APPENDIX A

———— ✻ ————

Numerous articles were published in newspapers and magazines beginning in 1986. The following pages are pertinent communications that can have been referenced in the book. They are in the order of dates written.

September 5, 1986: All Medicaid providers received this informational letter sent by the Ohio Department of Human Services.

October 20, 1989: I received this letter from Dr. Newman, Assistant Executive Director and Director of Legal and Regulatory Affairs, Practice Directorate of the APA.

December 1989: This article appeared in *Monitor* by James Bule: "Overzealous Medicaid investigation charged."

December 22, 1989: After the meeting in Washington, this letter was sent to Inspector General Richard P. Kusserow.

January 29, 1990: Dr. Newman received a response to the above letter.

February 1990: This article by Howard Fishman appeared in *The Psychiatric Times—Medicine & Behavior,* "Associations Unite to Look into Alleged Medicaid Fraud Investigation Abuses."

Spring 1990: Vol. 4, No. 1, This article was in the *Practice Directorate* (APA Publication): "Medicaid Fraud Cases on the Rise."

March 8, 1990: I received a letter from Betsy Ranslow, Administrative Director of the APA Office of Ethics.

March 21, 1990: This is my response to the above letter.

April 4, 1990: Betsy Ranslow acknowledged my response.

July 20, 1990: This is the informational bulletin letter from Dr. Bryant Welch, Executive Director for Professional Practice of APA.

Dated November 2, 1990: I sent this request letter I sent to Dr. Raymond Fowler, APA Chief Executive Officer, APA Psychology Defense Fund.

February 12, 1991: This is the denial response letter I received from Dr. Fowler.

From: Practice Directorate (APA Publication), Vol. 4, No. 1 – Spring 1990

Referral Services

22 State Associations Now Offering Service

A recent survey conducted by the Practice Directorate has determined that 22 state psychological associations currently maintain referral services for consumers seeking therapists in their areas.

Some of the survey results were extremely informative. For example, the survey showed that West Virginia, with approximately 460 providers, had the largest number of participating psychologists in its referral bank. The largest number of referral requests, however, came from Georgia—an average of 300 calls per month (the survey showed a 22-state referral average of 77 calls per month). Finally, the survey showed that the busiest time of year for the referral services was the pre- and post-winter holiday season, followed by the start of the school year.

The PD survey showed that successful referral services shared some common components, including:

- Organizing providers by both geographic location and area of specialty to speed response to caller requests;
- Offering three or four provider choices when possible, and then rotating names to the bottom of the list;
- Follow-up with both psychologist and potential patient to determine effectiveness of service;
- A fee or increased association dues for inclusion in service; and,
- Advertising of service in the Yellow Pages.

In addition to the components listed above, many referral services require participating providers to carry their own liability/malpractice insurance. Many services also issue a disclaimer at the time of referral, absolving the service of any responsibility for dissatisfaction with the provider.

According to the results, several other

Medicaid Fraud Cases on the Rise

Blame Laid on Overzealous Prosecutors and Unclear Regulations

Private practitioners face a dual problem when it comes to Medicaid fraud cases—overzealous prosecutors struggling to make their convictions quota, and unclear state Medicaid regulations. The combination of these two factors has led to an increase in the number of Medicaid fraud cases against mental health providers.

Ronald Schwartz, Health and Human Services deputy assistant inspector general, was recently quoted as saying, "More and more often, I believe, the emphasis is on statistics. State fraud units which have not produced lots of convictions have been put under terrific pressure." This new pressure, according

> "State fraud units...have been put under terrific pressure."

to a recent inspector general's report, has brought billions of dollars into the federal Treasury.

While Medicaid provisions may vary from state to state, there are a few basic prevention measures of which psychologists should be aware:

1. *Familiarize yourself with the terms of the agreement with Medicaid*—know what is expected in terms of record keeping, what information the agency will automatically have access to, etc.
2. *Have a thorough knowledge of billing procedures*. The rules governing

this may be very complex, but many of the cases filed have to do with inaccurate billing. Many practitioners leave this procedure up to support staff and fail to follow up to make sure the procedure is accurate. If you are confused by the rules, you should contact the responsible state agency to get

> *The rules governing this may be very complex, but many of the cases filed have to do with inaccurate billing.*

clarification or should consult with a knowledgeable attorney.

3. *Keep adequate records.*
4. *Keep a list of Medicaid clients*. You may want to keep a list of Medicaid clients so that, if agents request to view the files, there is no need to search through all files.

The rising number of claims against mental-health care providers was the subject of a recent meeting hosted by the APA Practice Directorate. Representatives of the American Psychiatric Association also attended the meeting.

APA and the American Psychiatric Association have agreed to create a joint educational campaign to alert members to problems with the fraud investigation procedures. Meetings with Department of Health and Human Services officials to clear up some of the ambiguous regulations also have been scheduled.

state associations were studying the feasibility of offering referral services. The PD recommends, however, that associations interested in referral services discuss their plans thoroughly with an attorney and an APA insurance representative. "There are a number of important policy issues to review before starting up a referral service," stated

Bryant Welch, J.D., Ph.D., executive director of the Practice Directorate. "Not only do these services require a great deal of staff support, but there are complex issues relating to liability, inclusion of non-association members and administrative costs."

For a copy of the state referral survey results, contact the Practice Directorate.

11

**American
Psychological
Association**

Advancing psychology as a science, a profession, and as a means of promoting human welfare

March 8, 1990

Mary D. Morgillo, Ph.D.   <u>CONFIDENTIAL</u>
1238 Millbury Road
Northwood, Ohio 43619

Dear Dr. Morgillo:

This is to notify you that the Ethics Committee of the American
Psychological Association, at its March 1-4, 1990 meeting, discussed the <u>sua
sponte</u> ethics complaint against you. Following this discussion and a full
review of the file, the Ethics Committee voted unanimously to find you in
violation of the following elements of the Ethics Code:

o   Principle 3.d, in that you pled guilty to one count of petty theft
     and "no contest" to two other counts of petty theft.

o   General Principle 1, in that by violating Principle 3.d you did
     not uphold the highest standards of the profession.

On the basis of the violations of General Principle 1 and Principle 3.d, the
Committee voted to Reprimand you and asked me to communicate to you its
concerns about your inadequate supervision. The Committee reminds you that
you are fully responsible for the services provided and the administrative
actions of your office.

We will need a letter from you within thirty days of your receipt of this
letter explicitly agreeing to accept the Reprimand. Upon receipt of such a
letter, the Committee will close the case with appropriate notification and
take no further action. We will, however, maintain the case file in
confidence for five years prior to destroying it. At that time, we will
maintain only a summary without identifying information for recordkeeping
and archival purposes.

Should you wish to appeal this decision, the Committee will expect a
statement from you, within the thirty day period, spelling out in detail
your reasons for nonacceptance.

Sincerely,

Betsy Ranslow
Administrative Director
Office of Ethics

BR:pag

1200 Seventeenth Street, N.W.

CHARLESGATE PSYCHOLOGICAL SERVICES, INC.

860 ANSONIA, SUITES 3 & 4
OREGON, OHIO 43616
MARY D. MORGILLO, PH.D., CLINICAL DIRECTOR

PSYCHOLOGICAL TESTING - PSYCHOTHERAPY
CONSULATATION SERVICES - HYPNOTHERAPY
STRESS MANAGEMENT - BIOFEEDBACK
(419) 698-1549
(419) 471-3217

March 21, 1990

Betsy Ranslow, Administrative Director
APA Office of Ethics
1200 Seventeenth Street, N.W.
Washington, D.C. 20036

Dear Ms. Ranslow:

In accordance with your request, this letter is to serve as an explicit

agreement on my part to accept the Reprimand as given by the Committee.

Sincerely,

Mary D. Morgillo, Ph.D., A.B.M.P.
Psychologist

MDM: x

107

**American
Psychological
Association**

Advancing psychology as a science, a profession, and as a means of promoting human welfare

April 4, 1990

Mary D. Morgillo, Ph.D.
1238 Millbury Road
Northwood, Ohio 43619

Dear Dr. Morgillo:

This is to acknowledge receipt of your letter of March 21, 1990 and your
acceptance of the Ethics Committee's decision to Reprimand you. I am now
closing this matter and will take no further action.

Consistent with Section 2.65 of the Rules and Procedures, the case file will
be maintained for five years after which only a summary, without identifying
information, will be kept for recordkeeping and archival purposes.

Thank you for your cooperation with this matter.

Sincerely,

Betsy Ranslow
Administrative Director
Office of Ethics

BR:pag

American
Psychological
Association

Advancing psychology as a science, a profession, and as a means of promoting human welfare

7/20/90

Dear Practitioner:

Last year, the APA Practice Directorate and many psychologists across the country worked successfully to secure a change in Federal law recognizing psychologists as providers eligible for direct reimbursement under the Medicare program. We are now entering the initial stages of implementation of the new law, and have recently received the first set of guidelines issued by Medicare to local insurance carriers on how to begin paying psychologists for diagnostic and therapeutic services rendered to Medicare beneficiaries.

The instructions, developed by the Health Care Financing Administration (HCFA) of U.S. Department of Health and Human Services, will give your local Medicare insurance carrier very basic guidance on how to pay psychologists under the new law, what services are covered and how they will be covered effective July 1, 1990. The instructions are not final regulations but do establish a system that will allow psychologists to begin billing for professional services until final rules are promulgated later this year.

While we were delighted with the passage of the Medicare legislation, we fully anticipated problems with implementation of the law. Historically, the Administration has not been supportive of the legislation. Moreover, organized psychiatry has continued efforts to dictate both the practice of psychology and the scope of the new law by lobbying HCFA to impede psychologists and their patients under the new statute.

The problems we anticipated were realized once HCFA began developing the instructions. The instructions contain a number of areas of concern, including certain restrictions on hospital inpatient billing and ambiguous language regarding the requirement that a psychologist confer with a patient's primary care physician.

The Practice Directorate is working to address these and other issues, and is now negotiating with the Administration for immediate change. We are also seeking an independent legal review of the instructions and are meeting with key Congressional offices to secure support for our position. If HCFA fails to make changes consistent with the scope and intent of the law, we will turn to legislative or judicial remedy.

1200 Seventeenth Street, N.W.
Washington, D.C. 20036
(202) 955-7600

109

While we continue to work with the Administration and our friends in Congress for change, you are free to exercise the rights you have been granted as an authorized provider under Medicare to treat Medicare beneficiaries within the scope of your state license. Attached is a summary of key features of the HCFA instructions to Medicare carriers, including telephone numbers of who to contact in your area for provider information to help orient you to the system.

It is also important for you to know that HCFA is beginning to pay greater attention to the area of fraud and abuse. We have become aware of increasingly intrusive investigations that are affecting greater numbers of mental health providers than ever before. Therefore, we urge you to become familiar with Medicare administrative procedures, keep accurate records, and speak frequently with local carriers and regional HCFA offices regarding your participation in the Medicare program.

We are sensitive to the added professional responsibilities you undertake if you choose to provide services under an insurance program as complex as Medicare. As such, we hope to assist you over the next several months by dedicating resources to disseminate information on the legal, professional, administrative, and clinical considerations in becoming a Medicare provider. The Practice Directorate will keep you and the State Psychological Associations apprised of our educational efforts as they develop.

Securing access to psychological care for those in need and ensuring the right for our profession to provide such services remains a major challenge. Our battle to obtain these goals in the Medicare program, for example, is not over. But with your continued support and patience, we can move toward removing other barriers to psychological care throughout our health care system.

Sincerely,

Bryant L. Welch, J.D., Ph.D.
Executive Director for
   Professional Practice

BLW/ba

THE NEW MEDICARE LAW FOR PSYCHOLOGISTS

WHAT THE LAW SAYS

Effective July 1, 1990, "qualified psychologists' services" are
reimburseable under Medicare Part B "as would otherwise be covered if
furnished by a physician or as an incident to a physician's services," if
the psychologist is practicing within the scope of state licensure laws.
The law also requires psychologists to "consult with the patients' primary
care physician," but only if the patient consents to such consultation.

The law removes the current $1375 annual cap for mental health services.
Psychologists will eventually be reimbursed under a fee schedule. Until
then, reimbursement is determined by local carriers. All mental health
benefits (including those provided by a psychiatrist) except initial
diagnostic tests are subject to a 50-50 copay: Medicare pays 50% and the
beneficiary pays 50%. Psychologists must accept the Medicare prescribed
rate (plus the beneficiary copay) as payment in full, and may not look to
the beneficiary or other sources to collect more (known as "mandatory
assignment").

HEALTH CARE FINANCING ADMINISTRATION (HCFA) GUIDELINES

HCFA recently issued "Carrier Manual Instructions" to implement the new law.
Next, HCFA will publish proposed rules for public comment, and then final
implementing rules which carry the force of law.

Under the instructions, psychologists may bill Medicare Part B directly for
outpatient testing and therapy services that the psychologist is eligible to
provide under state licensure laws. This includes services in nursing
homes, comprehensive outpatient rehabilitation facilities, community mental
health centers, private offices, and related outpatient settings. HCFA has
initially taken the position that psychologists may not bill Part B for
inpatient services, which HCFA claims are "rebundled" and reimburseable only
to the hospital under Part A. The Practice Directorate is presently engaged
in negotiations with HCFA to resolve this important issue favorably. In the
interim, the Practice Directorate cautions psychologists that billing
Medicare Part B directly for inpatient services will be problematic. In the
interim, they may wish to continue any existing arrangements with hospitals.

With regard to consultation, the Practice Directorate advises that
practitioners take the following steps:

1. Discuss with the patient the potential desirability of consulting with
   the primary care physician to consider potential medical problems;
2. Notify in writing or by telephone the patient's primary care physician
   that services are being provided, but only if the patient consents to
   such notification;
3. Document in the patient's chart that the patient was so advised, that
   such notification occurred, or that the patient did not want the primary
   care physician notified or consulted.

PSYCHOLOGISTS SHOULD CONTACT LOCAL CARRIERS (PHONE NUMBERS ENCLOSED) FOR
SPECIFIC INFORMATION REGARDING HOW TO BECOME A MEDICARE PROVIDER, BILLING
RATES, BILLING CODES, AND RELATED TECHNICAL INFORMATION, WHICH MAY VARY FROM
REGION TO REGION.

November 2, 1990

Raymond D. Fowler, Ph.D.
APA Chief Executive Officer
APA Psychology Defense Fund
1200 Seventeenth Street, N.W.
Washington, D.C. 20036

Dear Dr. Fowler:

I am writing this letter to request APA financial support in
bringing a constitutional challenge to the provision of federal law
by which the Inspector General of the U. S. Department of Health
and Human Services has imposed a five year exclusion against my
participation in Medicare and Medicaid. Several documents in
support of this request are enclosed and more specifically
described below.

FACTUAL BACKGROUND

In 1988 a "medifraud" investigation was initiated against me
based upon allegations made by an employee that I had terminated.
The terminated employee threatened legal action against my office
manager unless she cooperated and supported the allegations. (The
office manager has since admitted that such threats were made).
The office manager then signed an affidavit for a search warrant,
and a criminal investigation by the Lucas County Prosecutor ensued.

The essential conclusion of the investigation was that my
office manager, during two years of employment, had incorrectly
billed for certain services rendered, resulting in my having been
improperly reimbursed $1,910.00. (Incidentally, the investigation
also disclosed that the same office manager had failed to submit
claims for services valued at $9,000.00 for which I properly was
entitled to bill).

Only two improper billing practices were disclosed by the
investigation. First, if a patient did not appear for an
appointment, the patient was called, received a telephone session
of 45 minutes or more, and then Medicaid was billed for the
session. I was unaware the relevant regulations had changed and
that the client had to be personally in the office in order to
receive psychotherapy. It was my position that if the patient was

Raymond D. Fowler, Ph.D
November 2, 1990
Page - 2 -

unable to come in and a telephone session was needed, the service
was provided, and therefore properly billed.

Second, the office manager, who handled the submission of all
Medicaid claims, apparently did not know how to properly bill for
evaluations. Therefore, she had submitted claims for two to four
therapy sessions, rather than properly submitting claims for two to
four hours of psychological assessment. (She was aware that the
maximum number of hours that could be billed for psychological
testing per patient per year was four). At the same time, she
failed to bill for hospital evaluations I had conducted during the
period of her employment because she did not know the proper
coding.

The initial indictment against me was dismissed due to
prejudicial and abusive tactics by the prosecutor. However, in
order to bring to an end a protracted and nightmarish (and
financially draining) situation, I agreed to make an acknowledge-
ment that my employee had incorrectly submitted the claims; agreed
to reimburse the $1,910.00 that had been improperly submitted; and
agreed not to submit claims for the approximately $9,000.00 worth
of services that had not been billed, but which could have properly
been billed.

I further agreed to personally plead guilty to three counts of
petty theft in violation of Ohio Revised Code §2913.02(a),
misdemeanors of the first degree, as did the corporation through
which I did business, Charlesgate Psychological Services, Inc. The
prosecutor refused to accept a no contest plea and therefore both
I and the corporation were required to plead guilty in order to end
this very stressful and extraordinarily expensive process.
Attachment A. At the time I entered the plea I was advised that
under Ohio law my convictions would be expunged after one year.

On the same day I entered the guilty pleas (February 23, 1989)
I voluntarily submitted a letter on behalf of myself, and on behalf
of Charlesgate Psychological Services, Inc., to the Ohio Department
of Human Services, whereby I voluntarily canceled my participation
in the Ohio Medicaid program, which cancellation was understood by
me to be for a term of one year. See Attachment B.

Shortly thereafter I learned that the Inspector General was
considering further action. See Attachment C. My attorney, ████
████ provided a letter setting forth the circumstances of my
plea. See Attachment D.

On February 22, 1990, I was notified by the Office of the
Inspector General of the Department of Health and Human Services

Raymond D. Fowler, Ph.D
November 2, 1990
Page - 3 -

that I had been excluded from participation in the Medicare program as well as any state health care program, for a period of <u>five</u> years. See Attachment E. A similar notice was delivered to Charlesgate Psychological Services, Inc., dated March 1, 1990. See Attachment F. The notices stated that I could have a hearing with an administrative law judge, but could only question whether there were in fact convictions, and whether they related to the delivery of an item for service under Medicare or under any state health care program. Obviously, on these limited grounds any appeal would have been futile, and therefore none was pursued.

On June 6, 1990, my conviction, as well as that of Charlesgate Psychological Services, Inc., was expunged by the Common Pleas Court of Lucas County, Ohio. See Attachment G.

Notwithstanding the expungements, the five year exclusions remain in place. Based upon the five year exclusion imposed by the Inspector General, numerous third party providers have terminated my contracts. See, e.g., Attachments H and I.

The five year exclusion imposed by the Inspector General, combined with the resulting actions taken by third party providers, has totally destroyed my practice. I now have only ten clients, and am attempting to support myself and my husband, who suffered congestive heart failure last spring, by working part-time as an instructor at the Community and Technical College. My salary there is approximately $315.00, every two weeks until December 10, 1990, when the quarter ends. I have no additional employment prospects beyond that date. I have paid legal fees in excess of $22,000.00 to date, and have incurred additional costs associated with my defense of approximately $6,000.00. I have no additional resources available to me with which to mount a challenge to the five year exclusion imposed by the Inspector General.

I am now 56 years old. At no time throughout the course of this investigation was there ever a question raised about the quality of my clinical practice, my professional abilities, whether the services I rendered were appropriate, or whether or not the services were in fact given. Nonetheless, the conduct of the government combined with the mandatory five year exclusion imposed by current federal law, has totally destroyed my ability to earn a living. My husband can no longer work and I am the primary "breadwinner." His terminal condition and the additional medical expenses for this have added greatly to my emotional pain.

Raymond D. Fowler, Ph.D
November 2, 1990
Page - 4 -

PROPOSED LEGAL CHALLENGE

I have consulted with ████████████ of the firm of ████████████ in Toledo, Ohio. She advises me that because I entered into a plea bargain, there is now very little likelihood of successfully challenging that conviction, which the Inspector General is now using to deny me a livelihood. In hindsight, I realize that plea bargaining was a very foolish decision. I had no idea of the aftermath or consequences. I now must focus my attention on the extreme punishment that has been imposed as a consequence of the plea bargain, which I believe is greatly in excess of any that could be claimed as equitable even if the charges against me were accurate, which I vigorously deny.

At this point in time I would like to file a constitutional challenge to the mandatory five year exclusion contained in 42 U.S.C. §1320a-7(a), upon which the Inspector General has relied. The basis of that challenge is described in my counsel's letter of October 30, 1990, Attachment J. The costs of pursuing such an action are also described in the attachment.

I believe that such an action, if successful, would have value for all members of the APA. Recent publications are replete with accounts of prosecutorial misconduct with respect to medifraud investigations against psychiatrists and psychologists, as well as other medical providers. In the face of these onslaughts, the resulting stress and total disruption of one's life that results, and the incredible expense associated with mounting a defense, many persons have been psychologically beaten into submission and have entered guilty pleas to misdemeanors simply to avoid the cost (financial and emotional) of a jury trial. Under current law, such persons are then _automatically_ excluded from government reimbursement programs for five years, without any consideration for the surrounding circumstances, whether or not there was in fact culpability and intent, and irrespective of how small or how large the alleged loss of federal funds might be. Thus, we have situations such as mine where an individual pleads guilty to three misdemeanor offenses involving less than $900, but then is automatically excluded from any further participation in the programs for five years, thus totally ruining their professional practice.

I believe that this is fundamentally unfair and a violation of the right to due process of law protected by the United States Constitution. A challenge that successfully set aside the _mandatory_ five year exclusion would afford any person subsequently

Raymond D. Fowler, Ph.D
November 2, 1990
Page - 5 -

caught in this trap the opportunity to present mitigating and explanatory evidence and would permit the Inspector General to impose lesser periods of exclusion that reflect a greater fairness.

We all know that the instructions for submitting claims are ambiguous, and yet are used as proof of fraudulent billing when a medifraud unit initiates an investigation. The lack of intent to commit fraud is totally ignored. Nonetheless, many practitioners cannot afford the legal defense or the emotional costs of an investigation and are forced to lose their livelihood even when innocent, which is precisely what has happened to me. The legal challenge I propose would reduce the excessively harsh consequences that now result.

I urge your careful consideration of this request. If I can be of additional assistance, or can clarify any of the information contained in the attachments, please contact me at 419-698-1540. You may also feel free to contact my current attorney, ▓▓▓▓▓ ▓▓▓, or my trial attorney, ▓▓▓▓▓▓▓▓directly.

Sincerely,

Mary D. Morgillo, Ph.D., ABMP
Psychologist

American
Psychological
Association

Advancing psychology as a science, a profession, and as a means of promoting human welfare

February 12, 1991

Mary D. Morgillo, PhD
860 Ansonia, Suites 3 & 4
Oregon, OH 43616

Dear Dr. Morgillo:

Thank you for your application to the American Psychological Association (APA) Psychology Defense Fund (PDF). Your PDF application for a grant to help defray legal expenses associated with your defense of Medicaid fraud and abuse charges was considered by the Board of Directors during its February 6-7, 1991 meeting. I regret to inform you that the Board declined to approve your grant request.

Please recall that the PDF grant decisions are made by the Board of Directors following a review of the case based on criteria set forth by the Council of Representatives. The Board felt that a decision in your case would not necessarily be one that would be generalizable to the profession of psychology.

If you have any questions, please contact Cherie Mustico, PDF Coordinator, at 202/955-7647.

Sincerely,

Raymond D. Fowler, PhD
Chief Executive Officer

RDF/cm

cc: Russ Newman, PhD, JD
    Billy Hinnefeld, JD
    Cherie Mustico

1200 Seventeenth Street, N.W.
Washington, D.C. 20036

Richard F. Celeste
Governor

Ohio Department of Human Services

30 East Broad Street, Columbus, Ohio 43266-0423

September 5, 1986

Dear Medicaid Provider:

In May, Ohio Medicaid began to implement a new computerized claims processing system (the Medicaid Management Information System, or MMIS). Our former system had the dubious distinction of being the oldest MMIS in the country and was no longer capable of handling the large volume of claims we receive.

However the change to the new system inevitably has run into some temporary problems. There have been delays in the payment of some claims. Some claims have been rejected improperly. Providers trying to call us to register their complaints often found our phone lines tied up. Or they were promised that someone would call them back, but in fact no one called.

I am writing simply to let you know that we know these problems exist, and we are working as hard as we can to fix them. We have re-written some procedures, we have hired extra staff, and we have enhanced our phone capacity. None of this will undo the difficulties that some of you have encountered in the past, but it should give us a smooth running system in the future. Meanwhile, we ask you to bear with us.

The following information is provided in an effort to explain some of the difficulties and the steps we are taking to resolve them.

1. During the early days of implementation (May and June) a number of problems occurred relative to entering data into the system. Problem sources were varied and included scanner errors, incorrect keying instructions, and improperly completed claims. This caused thousands of claims to be rejected by the new system.

    We have been working to identify and re-enter those claims, but there remain a large number to be corrected. If you submitted claims in May and June about which you have heard nothing to date, we request that you not resubmit them at this time. Because we are now beginning to pay these claims, resubmittals could cause a duplication problem and lengthen reimbursement turnaround.

2. There are certain types of claims that we are having difficulty paying, but we are making changes on a daily basis in order to correct the system. Among the problem areas that we are working to resolve are Medicare crossover, pharmacy, ambulance, home health, and prior authorized procedures. Because it is important to make adjustments to the system in an orderly manner and test each major change thoroughly, problem resolution is rarely a quick process.

We are, however, taking a number of additional measures to move all claims through the system as swiftly as possible. These measures include reassigning and adding staff on a temporary basis to work on problem resolution, both for individual providers and for categories of claims.

3. Checks usually are mailed out within five working days, but recent mailing time has increased to approximately 10 working days. Steps are being taken to eliminate the backlog and reduce mailing time to its previous length.

4. When the new system was implemented, new claim forms were distributed to providers. A total of seven million forms was printed. Through a miscalculation, the department ran out of several types within a few months. Re-ordered forms have now been received by the ODHS forms distribution warehouse, and requests for all claim types are being filled.

5. Our Bureau of Provider Relations has been unable to keep up with the volume of provider inquiries generated by the new system, and we are in the process of making a number of changes aimed at increasing our responsiveness. If you have not received a reasonably prompt reply, we suggest that you address your reimbursement concerns to the bureau in writing rather than by phone.

We regret the difficulties experienced by providers during our transition to the new MMIS and intend to continue resolving them as quickly as possible.

Sincerely,

Paul Offner
State Medicaid Director

PO:kat

Advancing psychology as a science, a profession, and as a means of promoting human welfare

October 20, 1989

Mary D. Morgillo, Ph.D.
860 Ansonia, Suite #4
Oregon, OH 43616

Dear Dr. Morgillo:

On behalf of the American Psychological Association's (APA) Practice Directorate, thank you for taking the time to come to our offices for the meeting regarding Medicaid fraud investigations. Your participation furthered APA's understanding of the investigations and their problems. Our office is internally processing the wealth of information gathered from the meeting. I truly hope that a joint effort between the APA and the American Psychiatric Association can affect a remedy for the numerous problems with the system which were so articulately highlighted during the meeting.

Again, thank you for taking the time to travel to our offices.

Sincerely,

Russ Newman, Ph.D., J.D.
Assistant Executive Director
and Director of Legal and
   Regulatory Affairs
Practice Directorate

RN/cm

1200 Seventeenth Street, N.W.
Washington, D.C. 20036
(202) 955-7600

American
Psychological
Association

Advancing psychology as a science, a profession, and as a means of promoting human welfare

December 22, 1989

Richard P. Kusserow
Inspector General
Department of Health and Human Services
Room 5250
330 Independence Avenue SW
Washington, DC 20201

Dear Inspector General Kusserow:

On behalf of the American Psychological Association and the American
Psychiatric Association, we are taking this opportunity to bring to your
attention an apparently ongoing problem with possible abuses during
investigations by Medicaid Fraud Control Units. As a result of a series of
reports, meetings, and testimonials, our organizations are requesting a
meeting with your office to discuss the issues surrounding this problem.

As you may be aware, several psychologists and psychiatrists throughout
the nation have made allegations that during investigations of them by
Medicaid Fraud Control Units there have been various violations of
practitioners' and clients' civil rights. Some of these allegations have
actually led to lawsuits against certain states. For example, Carol Brown,
M.D., a psychiatrist in Hawaii, has brought suit against the state's
Department of Human Services and four state officials on the grounds of
infliction of emotional distress, breach of contract, negligent
administration of Medicaid, invasion of privacy, tortious interference with
contract, and civil rights violations. The suit was filed after she was
acquitted of 134 counts of Medicaid fraud.

Also in Hawaii, the American Civil Liberties Union testified before the
Hawaii legislature that "the Medicaid Fraud Control Unit has abused the
subpoena process and disregarded the privacy of people of this state."
Another similar case was filed in Hawaii by clinical psychologist Leonard
Licht. Dr. Licht was awarded $600,000 in damages for malicious prosecution.

In the cases reported to us or that we have learned of through other
means, certain themes can be found. These themes are:

1.   Apparent constitutional due process violations and harrassment by state
     investigators;

2.   Disregard for therapist-patient confidentiality by state investigators;

1200 Seventeenth Street, N.W.
Washington, DC 20036

121

Richard P. Kusserow
December 22, 1989
Page 2

3. Criminal fraud charges based on minor technical violations of the Medicaid procedures, such as coding errors by providers, or based on ambiguities of the Medicaid laws and regulations;

4. A resulting type of "double jeopardy" whereby providers are first prosecuted under criminal penalties followed by a similar process for civil penalties for the very same charges.

Since the federal Medicaid regulations (42CFR secs. 455.12 et. seq.) specifically provide that the methods used for investigating suspected fraud cases must not infringe on the legal rights of the persons involved and must afford due process of law, it must be assumed that your office would be concerned with the previously mentioned healthcare provider allegations. We would like to meet with you in hopes of promoting better understanding for all parties involved. We appreciate your time and consideration and look forward to hearing from you on this serious matter in the very near future.

Sincerely,

Russ Newman, Ph.D., J.D.
Assistant Executive Director
and Director of Legal and
 Regulatory Affairs
Practice Directorate
American Psychological Association

Jay B. Cutler, J.D.
Special Counsel, and
Director, Government Relations
American Psychiatric Association

cc: John M. Hamilton, M.D.
    Eugene D. Cassel

DEPARTMENT OF HEALTH & HUMAN SERVICES   Office of Inspector General

Washington, D.C. 20201

APA PRACTICE DIRECTORATE
LEGAL & REGULATORY AFFAIRS

JAN 2 9 1990

JAN 3 1 1990

Russ Newman, Ph.D., J.D.
Assistant Executive Director
Practice Directorate
American Psychological Association
1200 17th Street, N.W.
Washington, D.C. 20036

Dear Dr. Newman:

This is in response to your letter of December 22, 1989, in which
you expressed concerns about possible abuses during investigations conducted by Medicaid Fraud Control Units.

Your letter specifically mentioned cases of alleged abuse by the
Hawaii Medicaid Fraud Control Unit. Therefore, we have asked the
Attorney General of Hawaii, The Honorable Warren Price, III to
provide this office with all available information, and the
status and disposition of the cases. We have not as yet received
a reply.

When we receive the response from Attorney General Price, and
review the cases mentioned in your letter, we will be contacting
you to discuss your concerns. A copy of this letter will be sent
to Mr. J. B. Cutler, Special Counsel, American Psychiatric
Association, as he was a co-signatory of your letter.

                    Sincerely yours,

                    Richard P. Kusserow
                    Inspector General

cc:
The Honorable Warren Price, III

December 1989

Note: columns are continued on left page

Overzealous Medicaid investigations charged

By James Buie
Monitor staff

Indicted:

Genevieve Painter, an internationally prominent psychologist and author;

Richard Sword, a psychologist trying to help Vietnam veterans put their experiences of war behind them;

Leonard Licht, a psychologist in Hawaii and former assistant professor of psychiatry at the prestigious Albert Einstein College of Medicine in New York.

Painter, Sword and Licht were charged in the mid-1980s with criminal felonies for failing to follow the letter of state Medicaid regulations—regulations they considered vague and open to interpretation.

All three were ultimately cleared of the charges against them. Licht, in fact, has sued the state of Hawaii for "malicious prosecution" asking for $600,000 in damages. But their legal battles took an emotional, financial and professional toll that dozens of psychologists and other mental health professionals are facing in the 38 states where Medicaid fraud units have been established.

...that Medicaid fraud inves... s have harassed and ...dated them for making cler... rors or for misinterpreting ...uous Medicaid regulations. ...keswoman for the inspector ...al's office of the Health and ...n Services department ...d that its fraud squads have ...overzealously.

...fair prosecution of psycholo... ...nd other mental health ...sionals has been apparent ...least eight of the 38 states ...have established Medicaid ...control units, according to ...ard Fishman, a social worker ...has been investigating the ...lem for the last year in his ...city as associate editor of *Psychiatric Times*.

...shman has collected exam... of what he believes is unfair ...ecution of mental health pro... ...onals in states ranging from ...fornia to New York, and from ...to Texas. He has written six ...les on the issue that have run ...he front page of the psychi... ...trade newspaper. In October, ...rranged a meeting between ...viders accused of Medicaid ...d and leaders of the Amer... ...Psychiatric Association and ...American Psychological ...ociation to explore what might ...done about the problem on a ...ional basis.

"I've collected a file of more ...n 400 phone numbers of ...viders, attorneys, prosecutors, ...estigators," Fishman said from ...office in Mt. Airy, Md.

...very one of these people may ...guilty, but the question is, ...at are they guilty of? Tech... ...al violations. Using the wrong ...de. Not using the right date. ...ost of them had no intention at ...to defraud. You don't go ...ound destroying people's lives ...cause of that."

As a mental health profes-

could happen to anybody. It's an outrageous abuse of power."

Fishman described a typical pattern of abuse inflicted on mental health professionals by fraud investigators.

"The first thing a provider hears is from his patient. 'Doc, did you know these guys are out asking questions about you?'" Patient confidentiality is of little concern to the investigators, Fishman said. "They'll barge into a provider's office without a search warrant, with guns drawn, and riffle wholesale through confidential files of *all* the provider's patients."

A provider is then informed that his right to treat Medicaid or Medicare patients has been suspended pending investigation, Fishman said. Federal guidelines dictate that investigators first seek an informal inquiry, then an administrative hearing and arbitration, but these guidelines are often ignored, Fishman said. Little effort is made to protect a provider's right to due process or work the problem out administratively, he noted. Instead, the provider is slapped with heavy fines or a grand jury indictment for criminal fraud. And providers

civil courts for the same charges, Fishman said.

The problem looms larger now that psychologists seem likely to win inclusion as Medicare providers. Psychologists generally provide a relatively small volume of service for Medicaid, a state-run health care program for the poor and the homeless. But if Medicare covers psychological services, many psychologists may begin to treat a large number of elderly patients. And that means psychologists will have to confront and understand Medicare regulations, which could be just as complicated and ambiguous as state Medicaid rules.

"There's an enormous educational task confronting the profession of psychology," said Bryant Welch, executive director of the American Psychological Association's Practice Directorate. Psychologists' inclusion in Medicare will have a great positive impact on the profession, Welch said. "But many practitioners may understandably resent all the bureaucratic paperwork involved."

APA's Practice Directorate will work with the Health Care Financing Administration to see that Medicare regulations for psychologists are as straightforward as possible, Welch said. Given the reality of modern bureaucracy, however, practitioners should not expect a headache-free transition.

"The simple fact is that if we're going to participate in Medicare, we're going to have to learn the rules of the game," he said.

In state Medicaid programs, "it's clear psychologists are being victimized when they had no intention of doing anything immoral," Welch said. "Many of them were simply poorly informed about the nature of their obligations and liabilities."

tigators have been under pressure from state politicians, members of Congress and the U.S. Department of Health and Human Services (HHS) to pinpoint fraud, waste and abuse, and to increase conviction rates each year. The inspector general's office in HHS boasts that investigators saved the Medicare program $3 billion last year alone, and brought in more than 400 convictions for fraud, compared with 118 such convictions in 1987.

"We expect to increase that number substantially this year," said Judith Holtz, a public affairs officer for the inspector general's office.

But Holtz disputed charges that prosecutions have been unfair or malicious, or that the inspector general's office has intentionally rewarded employees for imposing penalties that have no merit.

"We deal with a half-million physicians plus a very large number of other providers," Holtz said. Four hundred convictions a year "hardly represents overzealous prosecution."

Holtz said she could not address specific cases of unfair

the white hats and are representing the best interests of U.S. taxpayers by preventing fraud and abuse," Holtz said.

But a number of psychologists, including Albert Lerner of Santa Rosa, Calif., have complained that Medicare and Medicaid fraud units "have been functioning as 'goon squads' and have used gestapo tactics to harass and destroy various therapists throughout the country." Lerner has been under investigation for Medicaid fraud since 1984. He said he has incurred more than $100,000 in legal expenses over the last five years and has been "both emotionally and financially devastated" by the investigation. To avoid further court costs and stress, he said, he pleaded guilty to one fraudulent claim of $51.60.

"Now I am faced with various administrative actions that threaten my license, membership in APA, my teaching credentials and my participation in Medicaid," Lerner said in a letter to *The Monitor*.

A psychologist from Ohio who attended the meeting with APA officials but asked not to be identified also complained of a "relentless, vindictive investigation" against her. In April of 1988, "two armed policemen, three undercover agents and a prosecuting attorney descended on my office with a search warrant," she said. She and her attorney remained optimistic that the investigation would not result in an indictment because "my records would show the allegations of fraud were false." But they were wrong.

She said she did not have the financial resources to continue fighting and is "giving in" by pleading guilty to several misdemeanor counts. That may lead to "an end to my career as a psy-

Photo by Rick Buell

Albert Lerner

Welch and Jay Cutler, director of governmental affairs for the American Psychiatric Association, have agreed to jointly petition HHS officials for a review of the questionable methods used by Medicaid and Medicare fraud investigators. They also said they will bring the

mittees. Both committed to work on producing handbooks for members clarifying Medicare and state Medicaid regulations.

APA's legal and regulatory affairs program is providing information for psychologists accused of Medicare or Medicaid fraud. "Psychologists must realize that they are up against a system that's out of whack," said Russ Newman, the program's director. "With health care and Medicaid costs skyrocketing, plus a small percentage of providers who may actually be attempting to defraud, investigators have the ill-conceived notion that their overzealous activity will somehow fix these problems."

Providers facing allegations of fraud "had better learn quickly that their rights, and perhaps even the rights of their patients, will not be taken for granted by investigators," Newman said.

Fishman said abusive prosecution was especially apparent in Hawaii, where for five years, the chief of the Medicaid fraud unit engaged in a "reign of terror" by prosecuting well-meaning health professionals for fraud. Ultimately, the convictions of dozens of health professionals were overturned, the chief of the Medicaid fraud unit resigned and the unit was all but disbanded.

But the fear that the investigations provoked in health professionals rivaled the fear one feels in a totalitarian state, said Leonard Licht.

"Many times throughout the process, I felt truth was irrelevant, in spite of the fact that I knew I had truth on my side," Licht said. "I was faced with an awesome political machine that made me feel like a helpless victim."

Licht was charged in 1985 with 14 counts of Medicaid fraud and one count of theft. He was

caid program of $1,600 becaus... he had allegedly failed to obtai... written referrals from physicia... to treat certain patients. Medicaid regulations did not state whether the referrals should be written or oral, Licht maintain... And he found himself victim o... personal vendetta from a psycl...

The fraud investigators "never would resolve the case administratively. They went directly into litigation, charging me with criminal intent," Licht said.

Licht was acquitted in 1985. He counter-sued. This year, a jury in the Second Circuit Court of Hawaii found that he had been a victim of malicious prosecution. In seeking an indictment against Licht, the Medicaid fraud chief had withheld "clearly exculpatory evidence" from the grand jury, and was "motivated by malice and not by an otherwise proper purpose," the jury concluded.

Licht is still waiting for the judge to rule on some of the changes in his suit. And his attorney expects the case will be appealed.

"I still feel a cloud hanging over my head," he said. The stress related to the case led to the breakup of his marriage and damaged his professional practice, he stated. "That feeling of powerlessness has left scars I still carry."

Two other Hawaii psychologists, Genevieve Painter and Richard Sword, were also scarred by the experience. Painter, author of several books, including *Teach Your Baby*, which was translated into eight languages and sold more than 150,000 copies, was indicted on 17 counts of failing to obtain a physician referral for Medicaid patients.

A meticulous record-keeper, Painter produced more than 100 copies of written referrals and hand-written notes of telephone referrals. With the help of a $15,000 grant from the APA's legal defense fund, she fought the state Medicaid system's charges for six years. Ultimately, she was acquitted on a technicality—"failure to obtain speedy justice."

"To be exonerated on a technicality," she said, "is scant

56　February 1990　　　　　　　　THE PSYCHIATRIC TIMES • MEDICINE & BEHAVIOR

Associations Unite to Look into Alleged Medicaid Fraud Investigation Abuses

by Howard Fishman

The national professional associations representing the majority of Medicaid and Medicare mental health providers have joined forces to look into Medifraud investigative abuses uncovered in five articles published by *The Psychiatric Times.* The American Psychiatric Association and the American Psychological Association have requested an opportunity to discuss their concerns about investigative practices with Richard P. Kusserow, inspector general of the Department of Health and Human Services, who is responsible for both the funding and monitoring of the Medicaid Fraud Control Units throughout the United States.

In addition, both of the associations have agreed to publish handbooks for their members detailing the responsibilities of Medicaid/Medicare providers and suggesting strategies for both

avoiding and coping with legal difficulties that may result from providing services under these programs. Both groups have also begun to address the issues in their newsletters and have designated staff members to respond to

members' complaints and concerns about the tactics used in fraud investigations.

The *Times* has arranged a meeting between providers accused of Medi-

caid fraud and leaders of the American Psychiatric Association and the American Psychological Association to explore what might be done about the problem on a national basis. The psychologists' publication, *The Monitor*

carried a report of the planned meeting in its January issue.

Abusive investigatory practices have been reported by practitioners to the *Times* in at least 10 of the 38 states where Medicaid fraud units have been established with federal funding. The states from which complaints have arisen are California, Hawaii, Massachusetts, Michigan, Minnesota, New Jersey, New York, Ohio, Oregon, and Utah. The allegations made by these providers against the Medicaid Fraud Control Units include denial of due process, intimidation of witnesses, subornation of testimony, breach of patient confidentiality, and entrapment.

> *The allegations made...against the Medicaid Fraud Control Units include denial of due process, intimidation of witnesses, subornation of testimony, breach of patient confidentiality, and entrapment.*

Letter Outlines "Themes"

The letter to Kusserow from the mental health organizations states: "In the cases reported to us or that we have learned of through other means, certain themes can be found." These themes are:

1. Apparent constitutional due process violations and harassment by state investigators;
2. Disregard for therapist-patient confidentiality by state investigators;
3. Criminal fraud charges based on minor technical violations of the Medicaid procedures, such as coding errors by providers, or based on ambiguities of the Medicaid laws and regulations;
4. A resulting type of "double jeopardy" whereby providers are first prosecuted under criminal penalties followed by a similar process for civil penalties for the very same charges.

"Since the federal Medicaid regulations specifically provide that the methods used for investigating suspected fraud cases must not infringe on the legal rights of the persons involved and must afford due process of law, it must be assumed that your office would be concerned with the previously mentioned healthcare provider allegations." The organized professional community has responded to these alleged abuses on a statewide basis in only a few previous instances. In a series of hearings before the Hawaii state legislature, the American Civil Liberties Union testified that "the Medicaid Fraud Control Unit (MFCU) has abused the subpoena process and disregarded the privacy of people of this state." The Hawaii Federation of Physicians and Dentists testified regarding "the MFCU's 'gestapo tactics' of bursting into offices with guns and without notice, removing files without permission, and prosecuting physicians for fraud involving small amounts of money for what physicians claim were billing errors or misunderstanding of Medicaid regulations."

In California, a Medi-Cal providers' organization was started several years ago, in part because of similar experiences with fraud investigators. The Illinois chapter of the American College of International Physicians "has taken an aggressive role in exposing the abuses of the civil rights of physicians and their patients by the State

Department of Public Aid," according to Kishore H. Thampy, M.D., the organization's president-elect.

The American Psychiatric Association has designated Jay B. Cutler, J.D., special counsel and director of government relations, to serve as its liaison to psychiatrists who have problems with Medicaid investigators. Similarly, psychologists have been encouraged to contact Russ Newman, Ph.D., J.D., assistant executive director and director of legal and regulatory affairs of the American Psychological Association.

Newman described the situation as "a system that's out of whack. With health care and Medicaid costs skyrocketing, plus a small percentage of providers who many actually be attempting to defraud, investigators have the ill-conceived notion that their overzealous activity will somehow fix these problems."

Bryant Welch, executive director of professional practice of the psychological association, stated that "it's psychologists are being victimized when they had no intention of doing anything immoral. Many of them are simply poorly informed about the nature of their obligations and liabilities."

Welch cited the *Times* "for the enormous service that you are providing to both psychologists and psychiatrists by your investigation of the Medicaid fraud issue. It was very opening for me, and I think you will find it is leading to a fairly comprehensive program to both educate and protect our members on the dangers of dealing with Medicaid patients."

Inspector General Kusserow was contacted several times for this article but declined comment.

Please see related article on page

APPENDIX B

———— ✳ ————

These are the prayers I would say every morning:

The Office of Christian Prayer: In June of 1976, I made a special retreat to begin my professional career in psychology. There, I dedicated myself to say the Office every morning and evening just as the priests and members of religious orders do.

Prayer to the Holy Spirit:

Come Holy Spirit, fill my heart with Your holy gifts. Let my weakness be penetrated with Your strength this very day that I may fulfill all the duties of my state conscientiously, that I may do what is right and just. Let my charity be such as to offend no one, and hurt no one's feelings; so generous as to pardon sincerely any wrong done to me. Assist me, O Holy Spirit, in all my trials of life, enlighten me in my ignorance, advise me in my doubts, strengthen me in my weakness, help me in all my needs, protect me in temptations and console me in afflictions. Graciously hear me, O Holy Spirit, and pour Your light into my heart, my soul, and my mind. Assist me to live a holy life and to grow in goodness and grace. Amen.

Consecration of the family to the Sacred Heart:

We consecrate to Thee, O, Jesus of love, the trials and the joys and all the happiness of our family life, and we beseech Thee to poor Thy blessings on all the members, absent and present, living and dead. And when, one after the other, we shall have fallen asleep in Thy Blessed Bosom, O Jesus, may all of us in Paradise find again our family united in Thy Sacred Heart. Amen.

Prayer to Our Blessed Mother:
Mother of sorrow, Mother of Christ, you had influence with your Divine Son when on earth, you have the same influence now in Heaven, please pray for me. Obtain from your Divine Son for me my request(s) if it be His Holy Will. O most beautiful flower of Mount Carmel, fruitful vine, splendor of Heaven, Blessed Mother of the Son of God, Immaculate Virgin, assist me in my necessity. (Make this nightmare be finished, help my parents and my family through this darkness, and give me the strength I need to survive it.) O Star of the Sea, help me and show me now that you are my Mother. Holy Mary, Mother of God, Queen of heaven and earth, I humbly beseech you from the bottom of my heart to secure for me my requests. There is no one that can withstand your power; show me herein that you are my Mother.

O Mary, who is conceived without sin, pray for me who has recourse to you. (Say three times.)

Sweet Mother, I put my causes in your hands. (Say three times.)

Prayer to the Blessed Virgin (by the Cure D'Ars):
O Thou Most Holy Virgin Mary, who dost evermore stand before the Most Holy Trinity, and to whom it is granted at all times to pray for us to Thy most Blessed Son; pray for me in all my necessities; help me, combat for me, give thanks for me, and obtain for me the pardon of all my sins. Help me especially at my last hour; and when I can no longer give any sign of the use of reason, then do thou encourage me, make the sign of the cross for me sprinkle me with holy water, and fight for me against the enemy. Make in my name a profession of faith, favor me with a testimony of my salvation; and never let me despair of the mercy of God. Help me to overcome the wicked enemy. And when I can no longer say "Jesus, Mary, Joseph, I place my soul in your hands," say it for me; and when I can no longer hear human words of consolation then do thou comfort me. Leave me not before I have been

judged; and if I have to expiate my sins in purgatory, (oh!) pray for me instantly, earnestly, and admonish my friends to procure for me a speedy enjoyment of the blessed sight of God. Lessen my sufferings, deliver me speedily and lead my soul into Heaven with thee, that united with all the elect I may there bless and praise my God and thyself for all eternity. Amen. (Say three "Hail Marys.")

During the afternoon, I would say my daily rosary, a daily devotional prayer, and read a section of the Bible.

At night, I would say the evening office, The Serenity Prayer, an act of contrition, and three Our Fathers for peace in my family, my country, and the world.

The Serenity Prayer:
GOD, grant me the serenity to accept the things I cannot change, courage to change the things I can, and the wisdom to know the difference. Living one day at a time; enjoying one moment at a time; accepting hardship as the pathway to peace. Taking, as He did, this sinful world as it is, not as I would have it. Trusting that He will make all things right if I surrender to His Will; that I may be reasonably happy in this life, and supremely happy with Him forever in the next. Amen

It was my prayers that kept me focused on the important things in life. Since I could not always have my Bible with me, I had my favorite Psalms and Passages in a folder with me. The following pages are the copies of what I carried with me.

PSALM 5 (2-8, 10-13):
Hearken to my words, O LORD; attend to my sighing. Heed my call for help, my king and my God! To you I pray, O LORD; at dawn you hear my voice; at dawn I bring my plea expectantly before you. For you, O God, delight not in wickedness; no evil (one) remains with you; the arrogant may not stand in your sight. You hate all evildoers; you destroy all who speak falsehood; the bloodthirsty and the deceitful the LORD abhors. ...For in their

mouth there is no sincerity; their heart teems with treacheries. Their throat is an open grave; they flatter with their tongue. Punish them O God; let them fall by their own devices; for their many sins, cast them out because they have rebelled against you. But let all who take refuge in you be glad and exult forever. Protect them, that you may be the joy of those who love your name. For you, O LORD, bless the just...; you surround (them) with the shield of your good will.

PSALM 10 (1-2, 12-15):
Why, O LORD, do you stand aloof? Why hide in times of distress? Proudly the wicked harass the afflicted, who are caught in the devices the wicked have contrived. ...Rise, O LORD! O God, lift up your hand! Forget not the afflicted! Why should the wicked man despise God, saying in his heart, "He will not avenge it"? You do see, for you behold misery and sorrow, taking them in your hands. ...Break the strength of the wicked and of the evildoer; punish their wickedness; let them not survive.

PSALM 13 (2-7):
How long, O LORD? Will you utterly forget me? How long will you hide your face from me? How long shall I harbor sorrow in my soul, grief in my heart day after day? How long will my enemy triumph over me? Look, answer me, O LORD, my God! Give light to my eyes that I may not sleep in death lest my enemy say, "I have overcome (her)"; lest my foes rejoice at my downfall though I trusted in your kindness. Let my heart rejoice in your salvation; let me sing of the LORD, "He has been good to me."

PSALM 35 (1, 4, 7-12, 19-29):
Fight, O LORD, against those who fight me; war against those who make war upon me. ...Let those be put to shame and disgraced who seek my life; let those be turned back and confounded who plot evil against me. ...For without cause they set their snare for me, without cause they dug a pit against my life. Let ruin come upon the unawares, and let the snare they have set catch them; into the pit they have dug let them fall. But I will rejoice in the LORD, I

will be joyful because of his salvation. All my being shall say, "O LORD, who is like you, the rescuer of the afflicted (mortals) from those too strong for (them), of the afflicted and the needy from their despoilers?" Unjust witnesses have risen up; things I knew not of, they lay to my charge. They have repaid me evil for good, bringing bereavement to my soul. ...Let not my undeserved foes wink knowingly. For civil words they speak not, but against the peaceful in the land they fashion treacherous speech. And they open wide their mouths against me, saying, "Aha, aha! We saw (her) with our own eyes!" You, O LORD, have seen; be not silent; Lord, be not far from me! Awake, and be vigilant in my defense; in my cause, my God and my Lord. Do me justice, because you are just, O LORD; my God, let them not rejoice over me. Let them not say in their hearts, "Aha! This is what we wanted!" Let them not say, "We have swallowed (her) up!" Let all be put to shame and confounded who are glad at my misfortune. Let those be clothed with shame and disgrace who glory over me. But let those shout for joy and be glad who favor my just cause; and may they ever say, "The LORD be glorified; he wills the prosperity of his servant!" Then my tongue shall recount your justice, your praise, all the day.

PSALM 36 (2-5):

Sin speaks to the wicked (ones) in (their) hearts; there is no dread of God before (their eyes), for (they) beguile (themselves) with the thought that (their) guilt will not be found out or hated. The words of (their) mouths are empty and false; (they have) ceased to understand how to do good. (They plan) wickedness in (their beds; they set) out on a way that is not good, with no repugnance for evil.

PSALM 37 (1-10):

Be not vexed over evildoers, nor jealous of those who do wrong; for like grass they quickly wither, and like green herbs they wilt. Trust in the LORD and do good, that you may dwell in the land and enjoy security. Take delight in the LORD, and he will grant you your heart's requests. Commit to the LORD your way; trust in him, and he will act. He will make justice dawn for you like the light; bright as the noonday shall be your vindication. Leave it to the LORD, and wait for him; be not vexed at the successful path of (those) who (do) malicious deeds. Give up your anger, and forsake wrath; be not vexed, it will only harm you. For evildoers shall be cut off, those who wait for the LORD shall possess the land. Yet a little while, and the wicked...shall be no more; though you mark (their places, they) will not be there.

PSALM 41 (5-13):

Once I said, "O LORD, have pity on me; heal me, though I have sinned against you. My enemies say the worst of me: "When will (she) die and (her) name perish?" When one comes to see me, he speaks without sincerity; his heart stores up malice; when he leaves he gives voice to it outside. All my foes whisper together against me; against me they imagine the worst: "A malignant disease fills (her) frame"; and "Now that (she) lies ill, (she) will not rise again." Even my friend, who had my trust and partook of my bread, has raised his heel against me. But you, O LORD, have pity on me, and raise me up, that I may repay them." That you love me I know by this, that my enemy does not triumph over me, but because of my integrity you sustain me and let me stand before you forever.

PSALM 52 (3-9):

Why do you glory in evil, you champion of infamy? All the day you plot harm; your tongue is like a sharpened razor, you practiced deceiver! You love evil rather than good, falsehood rather than honest speech. You love all that means ruin, you of the deceitful tongue! God himself shall demolish you; forever he shall break you; he shall pluck you from your tent, and uproot you from the land of the living. The just shall look on with awe; then they shall laugh at him: "This is the man who made not God the source of strength, but put his trust in his great wealth, and his strength in harmful plots."

PSALM 54 (3-9):

O God, by your name save me, and by your might defend my cause. O God, hear my prayer; hearken to the words of mouth. For haughty (human beings) have risen up against me and fierce (people) seek my life; they set not God before their eyes. Behold, God is my helper; the Lord sustains my life. Turn back the evil upon my foes; in your faithfulness destroy them. Freely will I offer you sacrifice; I will praise your name, O LORD, for its goodness. Because of all distress you have rescued me, and my eyes look down upon my enemies.

PSALM 55 (2-7, 17-29):

Hearken, O God, to my prayer; turn not away from my pleading; give heed to me, and answer me. I rock with grief, and am troubled at the voice of the enemy and the clamor of the wicked; for they bring down evil upon me, and with fury they persecute me. My heart quakes within me; the terror of death has fallen upon me. Fear and trembling come upon me, and horror overwhelms me, and I say, "Had I but wings like a dove, I would fly away and be at rest. ...But I will call upon God, and the LORD will save me. In the evening, and at dawn, and at noon, I will grieve and moan, and he will hear my voice. He will give me freedom and peace from those who war against me, for many there are who oppose me. God will hear me and will humble them from his eternal throne; for improvement is not in them, nor do they fear God.

PSALM 56 (2-14):

Have pity on me, O God, for (people) trample upon me; all the day they press their attack against me. My adversaries trample upon me all the day; yes, many fight against me. O Most High, when I begin to fear, in you will I trust. In God, in whose promise I glory, in God I trust without fear; what can flesh do against me? All the day they molest me in my efforts; their every thought is of evil against me. They gather together in hiding, they watch my steps. As they have waited for my life, because of their wickedness keep them in view; in your wrath bring down the peoples, O God. My wanderings you have counted; my tears are stored in your flask; are they not recorded in your book? Then do my enemies turn back, when I call upon you; now I know that God is with me. In God, in whose promise I glory, in God I trust without fear; what can flesh do against me? I am bound, O God, by vows to you; your thank offerings I will fulfill. For you have rescued me from death, my feet, too, from stumbling; that I may walk before God in the light of the living.

PSALM 57 (2-4):
Have pity on me, O God; have pity on me, for in you I take refuge. In the shadow of your wings I take refuge, till harm pass by. I call to God the Most High, to God, my benefactor. May he send from heaven and save me; may he make those a reproach who trample upon me; may God send his kindness and his faithfulness.

PSALM 58 (2-3, 11-12):
Do you indeed like gods pronounce justice and judge fairly, you (people) of rank? Nay, you willingly commit crimes; on earth you look to the fruits of extortion. ...The just man shall be glad when he sees vengeance; he shall bathe his feet in the blood of the wicked. And (people) shall say, "Truly there is a reward for the just; truly there is a God who is judge on earth!"

PSALM 59 (2-4, 13, 17-18):
Rescue me from my enemies, O my God; from my adversaries defend me. Rescue me from evildoers; from blood thirsty (people) save me. For behold, they lie in wait for my life; mighty (people) come together against me. Not for any offense or sin of mine, O LORD; By the sin of their mouths and the word of their lips let them be caught in their arrogance, for the lies they have told under oath. ...But I will sing of your strength and revel at dawn in your kindness; you have been my stronghold, my refuge in the day of distress. O my strength! Your praise will I sing; for you, O God, are my stronghold, my gracious God!

PSALM 62:
Only in God is my soul at rest; from him comes my salvation. He only is my rock and my salvation, my stronghold; I shall not be disturbed at all. How long will you set upon (me) and all together beat (me) down as though (I) were a sagging fence, a battered wall? Truly from my place on high they plan to dislodge me; they delight

in lies; they bless with their mouths, but inwardly they curse. Only in God be at rest, my soul for from him comes my hope. He only is my rock and my salvation, my stronghold; I shall not be disturbed. With God is my safety and my glory, he is the rock of my strength; my refuge is in God. Trust in him at all times, O my people! Pour out your hearts before him; God is our refuge! Only a breath are (mortals); an illusion are (persons) of rank; in a balance they prove lighter, all together, than a breath. Trust not extortion; in plunder take no empty pride; though wealth abound, set not your heart upon it. One thing God said; these two things which I heard; that power belongs to God, and yours, O Lord, is kindness; and that you render to everyone according to (their) deeds.

PSALM 64 (2-7):

Hear, O God, my voice in my lament; from the dread enemy preserve my life. Shelter me against the council of malefactors, against the tumult of evildoers, who sharpen their tongues like swords, who aim like arrows their bitter words, shooting from ambush at the innocent (ones), suddenly shooting at (them) without fear. They resolve on their wicked plan; they conspire to set snares, saying, "Who will see us?" They devise a wicked scheme, and conceal the scheme they have devised; deep are the thoughts of each heart.

PSALM 69 (4-5, 14, 17-21):

I am wearied with calling, my throat is parched; my eyes have failed with looking for my God. Those outnumber the hairs of my head who hate me without cause. Too many for my strength are they who wrongfully are my enemies. Must I restore what I did not steal? ...But I pray to you, O LORD, for the time of your favor, O God! In your great kindness answer me with your constant help. ... Answer me, O LORD, for bounteous is your kindness; in your great mercy turn toward me. Hide not your face from your servant; in my distress, make haste to answer me. Come and ransom my life; as an answer for my enemies, redeem me. You know my reproach, my shame and my ignominy; before you are all my foes. Insult has broken my heart, and I am weak; I looked for sympathy, but there was none; for comforters, and I found none.

PSALM 70:

Deign, O God, to rescue me; O LORD, make haste to help me. Let them be put to shame and confounded who seek my life. Let them be turned back in disgrace who desire my ruin. Let them retire in their shame who say to me, "Aha, aha!" But may all who seek you exult and be glad in you, and may those who love your salvation say ever, "God be glorified!" But I am afflicted and poor; O God, hasten to me! You are my help and my deliverer; O LORD, hold not back!

PSALM 73 (1-4, 12-17, 23-24, 27):

How good God is to the upright; the LORD, to those who are clean of heart! But, as for me, I almost lost my balance; my feet all but slipped, because I was envious of the arrogant when I saw them prosper though they were wicked. For they are in no pain; their bodies are sound and sleek.... Such, then, are the wicked; always carefree, while they increase in wealth. Is it in vain I have kept my heart clean and washed my hands as an innocent (woman)? For I suffer affliction day after day and chastisement with each new dawn. Had I thought, "I will speak as they do," I had been false to the fellowship of your children. Though I tried to understand this it seemed to me too difficult, till I entered the sanctuary of God and considered their final destiny. ...Yet with you I shall always be; you have hold of my right hand; with your counsel you guide me, and in the end you will receive me in glory. ...For indeed, they who withdraw from you perish; you destroy everyone who is unfaithful to you.

PSALM 86 (7, 16-18):

In the day of my distress I call upon you, for you will answer me. ...Turn toward me, and have pity on me; give your strength to your servant.... Grant me a proof of your favor, that my enemies may see, to their confusion, that you, O LORD, have helped and comforted me.

PSALM 88 (2-5):

O LORD, my God, by day I cry out, at night I clamor in your presence. Let my prayer come before you; incline your ear to my call for help, for my soul is surfeited with troubles and my life draws near to the nether world. I am numbered with those who go down into the pit; I am a (woman) without strength.

PSALM 94 (16-23):

Who will rise up for me against the wicked? Who will stand by me against the evildoers? Were not the LORD my help, I would soon dwell in the silent grave. When I say, "My food is slipping," your kindness, O LORD, sustains me; when cares abound within me, your comfort gladdens my soul. How could the tribunal of wickedness be leagued with you, which creates burdens in the guise of law? Though they attack the life of the just and condemn innocent blood, yet the LORD is my stronghold, and my God the Rock of my refuge. And he will require them for their evildoing, and for their wickedness he will destroy them; the LORD, our God, will destroy them.

PSALM 109 (1-5, 21-29):

O God, whom I praise, be not silent, for they have opened wicked and treacherous mouths against me. They have spoken to me with lying tongues, and with words of hatred they have encompassed me and attacked me without cause. In return for my love they slandered me but I prayed. They repaid me evil for good and hatred for my love. ...But do you, O GOD, my Lord, deal kindly with me for your name's sake; in your generous kindness rescue me; for I am wretched and poor, and my heart is pierced within me. Like a lengthening shadow I pass away; I am swept away like the locust. My knees totter from my fasting, and flesh is wasted of its substance. And I am become a mockery to them; when they see me, they shake their heads. Help me, O LORD, my God; save me, in your kindness, and let them know that this is your hand; that you, O LORD, have done this. Let them curse, but do you bless; my adversaries be put to shame, but let your servant rejoice.

Let my accusers be clothed with disgrace and let them wear their shame like a mantle.

PSALM 142:

With a loud voice I cry out to the LORD; with a loud voice I beseech the LORD. My complaint I pour out before him, before him I lay bare my distress. When my spirit is faint within me, you know my path. In the way along which I walk they have hid a trap for me. I look to the right to see, but there is no one who pays me heed. I have lost all means of escape; there is no one who cares for my life. I cry out to you, O LORD, I say, "You are my refuge, my portion in the land of the living." Attend to my cry, for I am brought low indeed. Rescue me from my persecutors, for they are too strong for me. Lead me forth from prison, that I may give thanks to your name. The just shall gather around me when you have been good to me.

WISDOM 3 (9-11), 5 (16-17):

They that trust in him shall understand the truth: and they that are faithful in love shall rest in him: for grace and peace is to his elect. But the wicked shall be punished according to their own devices: who have neglected the just, and have revolted from the Lord. For he that rejecteth wisdom, and discipline, is unhappy: and their hope is vain, and their labors without fruit, and their works unprofitable.

But the just shall live for evermore: and their reward is with the Lord, and the care of them with the most High. Therefore shall they receive a kingdom of glory and a crown of beauty at the hand of the Lord: for with his right hand he will cover them, and with his holy arm he will defend them.

ECCLESIASTICUS 6 (1-15):

Instead of a friend, become not an enemy to the neighbor: for an evil man shall inherit reproach and shame. So shall every sinner that is envious and double tongued. Extol not thyself in the thoughts of thy soul like a bull: lest thy strength be quashed by folly, and it eat up they leaves, and destroy thy fruit, and thou be left as a dry tree in the wilderness. For a wicked soul shall destroy him that hath it, and maketh him to be a joy to his enemies, and shall lead him into the lot of the wicked. A sweet word multiplieth friends and appeaseth enemies, and a gracious tongue in a good man aboundeth. Be in peace with many, but let one of a thousand be thy counsellor. If thou wouldst get a friend, try him before thou takest him, and do not credit him easily. For there is a friend for his own occasion, and he will not abide in the day of thy trouble. And there is a friend that turneth to enmity; and there is a friend that will disclose hatred and strife and reproaches. And there is a friend, a companion at the table, and he will not abide in the day of distress. A friend, if he continue steadfast, shall be to thee as thyself, and shall act with confidence among them of thy household. If he humble himself before thee, and hide himself from thy face, thou shalt have unanimous friendship for good. Separate thyself from thy enemies, and take heed of thy friends. A faithful friend is a strong defense: and he that hath found him hath found a treasure. Nothing can be compared to a faithful friend, and no weight of gold and silver is able to countervail the goodness of his fidelity.

JEREMIAS 11 (18-20, 22-23):
But thou, O Lord, hast shown me, and I have known: then thou showedst me their doings. And I *was* as a meek lamb that is carried to be a victim: and I knew not that they had devised counsels against me, saying: Let us put wood on his bread, and cut him off from the land of the living, and let his name be remembered no more. But thou, O Lord of Sabaoth, who judgest justly, and triest the reins and the hearts, let me see thy revenge on them: for to thee have I revealed my cause. ...Therefore thus saith the Lord of hosts: Behold I will visit upon them: ...for I will bring in evil upon (them)....

MATTHEW 5 (43-48):
"You have heard that it was said, 'Thou shalt love thy neighbor, and shalt hate thy enemy.' But I say to you, love your enemies, do good to those who hate you, and pray for those who persecute and calumniate you, so that you may be children of your Father in

heaven, who makes his sun to rise on the good and the evil, and sends rain on the just and the unjust. For if you love those that love you, what reward shall you have? Do not even the publicans do that? And if you salute your brethren only, what are you doing more than others? Do not even the Gentiles do that? You therefore are to be perfect, even as your heavenly Father is perfect."

JOHN 15 (18-19):

"If the world hates you, know that it has hated me before you. If you were of the world, the world would love what is its own. But because you are not of the world, but I have chosen you out of the world, therefore the world hates you."

ROMANS 2 (1-2, 6-11):

Wherefore, thou are inexcusable, O man, whoever thou art who judgest. For wherein thou judgest another, thou dost condemn thyself. For thou who judgest doest the same things thyself. And we know that the judgment of God is according to truth against those who do such things.... God) will render to every man according to his works. Life eternal indeed He will give to those who by patience in good works seek glory and honor and immortality; but wrath and indignation to those who are contentious, and who do not submit to the truth but assent to iniquity. Tribulation and anguish shall be visited upon the soul of every man who works evil.... But glory and honor and peace shall be awarded to everyone who does good....

ROMANS 12 (9-21):

Let love be without pretense. Hate what is evil, hold to what is good. Love one another with fraternal charity, anticipating one another with honor. Be not slothful in zeal; be fervent in spirit, serving the Lord, rejoicing in hope. Be patient in tribulation, persevering in prayer. Share the needs of the saints, practicing hospitality. Bless those who persecute you; bless and do not curse. Rejoice with those who rejoice; weep with those who weep. Be of one mind towards one another. Do not set one mind towards one another. Do not set your mind on high things but condescend to the lowly. Be not wise in your conceits. To no man render evil for evil, but provide good things not only in the sight of God, but also in the sight of all men. If it be possible, as far as in you lies, be at peace with all men. Do not avenge yourselves, beloved, but give place to the wrath, for it is written, "Vengeance is mine; I will repay, says the Lord." But "If thy enemy is hungry, give him food; if he is thirsty, give him drink; for by so doing thou wilt heap coals of fire upon his head." Be not overcome by evil, but overcome evil with good.

ROMANS 14 (12-13, 16-19):

Therefore every one of us will render an account for himself to God. Therefore let us no longer judge one another, but rather judge this, that you should not put a stumbling block or a hindrance in your brother's (or sister's) way. ...Let not, then, our good be reviled. For the kingdom of God does not consist in food and drink, but in justice and peace and joy in the Holy Spirit; for he who in this way serves Christ pleases God and is approved by men. Let us, then, follow after the things that make for peace, and let us safeguard the things that make for mutual edification.

ROMANS 16 (17-20):

Now I exhort you, brethren, that you watch those who cause dissensions and scandals contrary to the doctrine that you have learned, and avoid them. For such do not serve Christ our Lord but their own belly, and by smooth words and flattery deceive the hearts of the simple. For your submission to the faith has been published everywhere. I rejoice therefore over you. Yet I would have you wise as to what is good, and guileless as to what is evil. But the God of peace will speedily crush Satan under your feet. The grace of our Lord Jesus Christ be with you.

GALATIANS 2 (16):

But we know that man is not justified by the works of the Law, but by the faith of Jesus Christ. Hence we also believe in Christ Jesus, that we may be justified by the faith of Christ, and not by the works of the Law; because by the works of the Law no man will be justified.

II TIMOTHY 2 (8-13):

Remember that Jesus Christ rose from the dead and was descended from David; this is my gospel, in which I suffer even to bonds, as a criminal. But the word of God is not bound. This is why I bear all things for the sake of the elect, that they also may obtain the salvation that is in Christ Jesus, with heavenly glory. This saying is true: If we have died with him, we shall also live with him; if we endure, we shall also reign with him; if we disown him, he also will disown us; if we are faithless, he remains faithful, for he cannot disown himself.

II TIMOTHY 4 (6-8, 16-17):

As for me, I am already being poured out in sacrifice, and the time of my deliverance is at hand. I have fought the good fight, I have finished the course, I have kept the faith. For the rest, there is laid up for me a crown of justice, which the Lord, the just Judge, will give to me in that day; yet not to me only, but also to those who love his coming. ...At my first defense no one came to my support, but all forsook me, may it not be laid to their charge. But the Lord stood by me and strengthened me....

I PETER 3 (8-17):

Finally, be all like-minded, compassionate, lovers of the brethren, merciful, humble; not rendering evil for evil, or abuse for abuse, but contrariwise, blessing; for unto this were you called that you might inherit a blessing. For, "he would love life, and see good days, let him refrain his tongue from evil, and his lips that they speak not deceit. Let him turn away from evil and do good, let him seek after peace and pursue it. For the eyes of the Lord are upon the just, and his ears unto their prayers; but the face of the Lord is against those who do evil." ...And who is there to harm you, if you are zealous for what is good? But even if you suffer anything for justice' sake, blessed are you. So have no fear of their fear and do not be troubled. But hallow the Lord Christ in your hearts. Be ready always with an answer to everyone who asks a reason for the hope that is in you. Yet do so with gentleness and fear, having a good conscience, so that wherein they speak in disparagement of you they who revile your good behavior in Christ may be put to shame. For it is better, if the will of God should so will, that you suffer for doing good than for doing evil.

II PETER 2 (1-3, 8-10, 21):

But there were false prophets also among the people, just as among you there will be lying teachers who will bring in destructive sects. They even disown the Lord who bought them, thus bringing upon themselves swift destruction. And many will follow their wanton conduct, and because of them the way of truth will be maligned. And out of greed they will with deceitful words use for their gain. Their condemnation, passed of old, is not made void, and their destruction does not slumber.... For by what that just man saw and heard while dwelling among them, they tormented his just soul day after day with their wicked deeds. The Lord knows how to deliver the God-fearing from temptation and to reserve the wicked for torment on the day of judgment, but especially those who follow the flesh in unclean lust and despise authority. ...For it were better for them not to have known the way of justice, than having known it, to turn back from the holy commandment delivered to them.

CPSIA information can be obtained
at www.ICGtesting.com
Printed in the USA
FFHW021428281118
49686078-54063FF